WHAT PEOPLE ARE SAYING ABOUT *THE GUILT TRAP*

"Dr. Lasson demonstrates the rare combination of clinician acumen, sense of humor, and humane compassion for the individuals in his care. *The Guilt Trap* is a source of encouragement and inspiration for all who face the challenges of working with similar populations."
—Rabbi Dr. Tzvi Hersh Weinreb, Executive Vice President Emeritus, Orthodox Union; Editor-in-Chief, *Koren Talmud Bavli*; Author, *Person in the Parasha*

"In *The Guilt Trap and Other Tales of Psychotherapy*, Dr. Lasson presents a vivid demonstration of what can actually happen in the therapy office. With compassion and humor, Dr. Lasson brings out the glory and drama that comes with being a therapist. A must-read for up and coming therapists as well as anyone who would like to be a 'fly on the wall' inside a skilled therapist's office."
—Dr. David Lieberman, world-renowned psychologist, public speaker and author of *Never Get Angry Again* and *Make Peace with Anyone*

"Understanding the meaning of guilt in our daily life can be a powerful source of growth, insight, and self-awareness. In *The Guilt Trap and Other Tales of Psychotherapy*, Dr. Jonathan Lasson has illuminated the many ways that understanding the role of guilt and its various manifestations can serve as a roadmap to improving the quality of our relationship with ourselves and others. Dr. Lasson models how he has grown from honestly confronting various challenges, successes and failures in his professional life. He skillfully uses powerful stories to illustrate his personal experiences as a therapist, drawing us into a deeper understanding of how therapy can make our lives better. I recommend this book to anybody who is interested in attaining a deeper understanding of the therapeutic process and insight into the process of change."

—Dr. David Pelcovitz, Straus Chair in Psychology and Education, Yeshiva University

THE
GUILT TRAP
AND OTHER TALES
OF PSYCHOTHERAPY

DR. JONATHAN M. LASSON

LEV AVOS PRESS
BALTIMORE, MARYLAND

Lev Avos Press
6210 Benhurst Road
Baltimore, Maryland 21209
doctorjonny.com

All names and identifying characteristics contained within the book content—including exact physical locations, occupations and other details—have been changed.

Cover design and interior layout design:
Ruth Schwartz, TheWonderlady.com

Ordering Information:
Quantity sales. Special discounts are available on quantity purchases by corporations, associations, and others. For details, contact the "Special Sales Department" at the address above.

The Guilt Trap and Other Tales of Psychotherapy /
Dr. Jonathan M. Lasson—1st ed.
978-0-9991309-0-2 paperback edition
978-0-9991309-1-9 ebooks edition
Library of Congress Control Number: 2017949754

This book is dedicated to my parents, wife and children and to all those who have guided me and allowed me to guide them in life.

TABLE OF CONTENTS

Introduction 1

My First Client Ever 9

Walk the Walk and Talk the Talk 15

What's That Fool Thing on Your Head? 27

Therapy or Confession 39

Narcissism and Wooden Ducks 49

Small Doses 57

Do You Know the Greenbaums? 67

I'm at Your Front Door 75

Car Washes 85

I'm Glad I Cured You 95

Caught in a Guilt Trap 101

I Don't Like Happy Therapists 109

The Old Warrior 125

Am I on *The Wire*? 133

You're a Racist! 145

Anime Abe 155

The Lonely Genius 165

Streaming and Dreaming 175

No Music Therapy Allowed! 183

Religious Guilt 187

Afterword 195

A note to readers struggling with unresolved guilt 205

A note to clinicians dealing with unresolved "therapist guilt" 211

Acknowledgments 217

INTRODUCTION

The phone call came from a rabbi friend of mine. "Joe is dead, and they believe it was a suicide." My reaction was typical for my personality. I asked the rabbi some basic questions, expressed my sympathies without becoming overly emotional, and then I obsessed.

Joe had been a client of mine for close to a year. It all began with some testing required by Joe's school because he was having difficulties, both academically and socially. The testing revealed that Joe possessed superior intelligence, but he also had a strong tendency to misread social cues.

This led to social alienation and feelings of inferiority. Joe was becoming more and more reserved, which concerned his parents to the point of referring him for therapy. His interests had become narrower, and he seemed to take very little pleasure in activities that he once enjoyed. His siblings and friends had also noticed the change but were too afraid or ambivalent to get involved.

It appeared that Joe was improving with process-oriented therapy. In fact, the last time I saw him he looked better than ever. He had a spring in his step, dressed more fashionably, and seemed surprisingly calm, which was a stark contrast to the overly anxious Joe whom I had been treating for the past year. I should have taken that as a warning sign, but I made the cardinal mistake that many colleagues in the field make when assessing suicide risk. I interpreted his calm as a sign that he had made a miraculous recovery. In reality, the calm was most probably due to the fact that he had made up his mind to end his life and was now comfortable with his decision.

As a therapist, and I can only speak for myself, I felt woefully unprepared for the guilt feelings that would consume me. I felt I should have done something different, a feeling therapists must confront after something drastic happens like the suicide of a patient. In my case this was certainly true. In hindsight, I second-guessed myself and said all the common things that therapists think about after a suicide. How come I did not recognize the signs earlier on? I should have increased the number of sessions per week. I should have put together an anti-suicide contract. The guilt factor certainly plays a role in a therapist's life. It can lead a therapist to question his abilities and, in some cases, leave the profession altogether.

Informal conversations with my colleagues have led me to believe that post-suicide guilt is one of the most significant, if not the major, area of guilt that we experience as mental health providers. Of course, suicide isn't the only cause of our guilt. My colleagues and I have talked about feeling guilty because we weren't fully paying attention during sessions, showing up late for sessions, having either positive or negative thoughts about our clients during sessions that were not germane to the content and feeling guilty for billing for missed sessions.

This sense of toxic therapist guilt might be the direct result of unresolved guilt feelings that have permeated the minds of therapists and counselors throughout time. Therapists are human. We make mistakes. We feel guilty. Giving the wrong advice is almost never an intentional act.

However, we tend to second-guess ourselves when things do not work out well for our clients, and we breathe a sigh of relief when our clients improve based on our therapeutic techniques.

Take, for example, Dr. Tim Smith, a clinical psychologist with over ten years of experience. All throughout his practice, Dr. Smith felt very confident about his abilities and received many compliments and positive feedback from his clients. Then one day he received a call from the distraught mother of a seventeen-year-old girl who was hospitalized after she overdosed on barbiturates. She later died after not waking from her comatose state. A suicide note was left in her bedroom. The mother was calling to inform Dr. Smith of her daughter's passing, and she wanted to reassure him that there was nothing he could have done to prevent her daughter's suicide. She just wanted to thank him for trying. It does not always work out that a parent will call to assuage the guilt of the therapist. Most therapists will experience a guilt that is similar to post-traumatic stress disorder (PTSD), with flashbacks to previous sessions and the compensatory actions that follow the obsessive thoughts that are often self-destructive in nature.

Guilt is a powerful emotion for all of us. When I began this book, I meant to write specifically on the topic of guilt. I conducted a pilot study and constructed a guilt scale consisting of more than forty-five items related to an individual's experience with guilt.

From the sampling of responses I received in the initial phase of the survey, it was clear how personal guilt really is. What one might deem worthy of guilt feelings others see as a waste of emotional energy. It is also interesting to see the different reflections on guilt between those who are religious and those who are not.

I began writing a story about a client suffering from religious guilt, and as time went by, a new idea formulated in my mind. I decided that readers would benefit more from a narrative than from a clinical presentation and research-based approach to understanding guilt.

Over the summer of 2016, I wrote about people with whom I have worked over the past twenty years. These are individual stories whose common thread is issues that negatively affect the human condition. Guilt certainly plays a role for many of my clients—and their stories often interweave feelings of guilt. But their issues span a range of emotions, from guilt and depression to narcissism and obsession.

When I think back to my first experiences with guilt, I realize how I utilized the self-destructive form of guilt to guide me, even as a young boy. I consider myself to be a pretty law-abiding citizen. However, as a guilt-minded person, I did not have to think long and hard about my first incident breaking the law. I believe it was the last incident as well.

When I was about twelve years old, I was with a friend of mine at a drugstore in Baltimore, where I grew up. My friend Jake, who was more daring than I, had what we can call a "sticky finger" problem. On one particular day, Jake dared me to steal a pack of baseball cards from the drugstore. In an attempt to win his approval, I quietly slipped the pack into my pocket. I left the shop with my friend and a pack of cards I had not paid for. At first, I felt a slight thrill because I had stolen without getting caught. However, it did not take long before the guilt set itself into full motion.

For the next few months, I avoided that drugstore, believing that the store owner must know that I had taken the baseball cards. I felt I had become a bad person by committing that crime.

As the day of my Bar Mitzvah drew near, I was sitting in a Jewish ethics class. The teacher read a passage from the Talmud stating you should return that which you have stolen, even if the incident occurred a long time ago. I felt as though he were speaking directly to me and knew exactly what I had done. This was obviously not the case, just the product of my guilty conscience.

I tried to put the incident out of my mind and vowed never to commit an act of theft again. However, the guilt kept plaguing me. It reached its pinnacle after hearing another talk in synagogue about being honest and responsible in all your actions. How could I feel like a good, maturing young adult when I knew I had wronged someone? So, with all the courage I could muster, I went back to the drugstore to find the store owner.

I asked if I could speak with him privately. I told him about the crime I had committed a few months earlier and, placing a dollar on his desk, said that I wanted to pay him for the package of cards. He assured me that I had done the right thing by paying for it, but he did not think that the cards were worth more than a quarter. I asked him to forgive me because the next month I was having my Bar Mitzvah and I wanted to start my account with God with a clean slate. He smiled, patted me on the head, and said, "Apology accepted." I walked away feeling greatly relieved.

An act such as this comes with a commitment. When a person goes public with his or her misdeeds, he becomes bound to his promise. I became bound to my commitment and avoided even a twinge of guilt associated with theft. I became overly conscientious when a cashier gave me more change than required. I would also make sure that my friends did the same. In a way, I became obsessed with honesty.

You may ask, what can be wrong with that? Well, as I mentioned before, it comes with a price. Becoming obsessed with a positive quality such as honesty can lead to self-destructive feelings and compulsive double-checking to be sure you have been scrupulous. There has to be a balance. Over the years I have settled down, but I am still known to be overly scrupulous in certain areas.

My friend Jake, did not fare as well. Once a person engages in a crime multiple times without guilt, he is destined to engage in further antisocial behaviors. The Talmud calls this phenomenon the "as if it becomes permissible" phenomenon. Jake did not see the big deal in taking small items that did not belong to him and eventually escalated his antisocial behaviors to larger things such as stealing cars and scamming people out of their hard-earned money. He ended up becoming a frequent flyer in the Maryland prison system. In some ways, I was envious of Jake at the time because he was not a worrier like I was, but I realized also that there must be a balance. My guilt could be as self-destructive as Jake's lack of guilt was destructive to others.

The stories in this book are not all related to guilt, but one can make the argument that there is an element of guilt in everyone's story. As a mental health professional, I hear stories every day that are unique to each person. Yet our stories connect us. Hearing others' experiences illuminates our understanding and can help us better understand our own behaviors and feelings.

Sharing these stories offers a glimpse into what therapists and counselors encounter in our work with clients. I hope that these tales of psychotherapy succeed in inspiring a younger generation of therapists with an "out of the box" approach. I also hope that other readers will be able to relate to some of the individuals who have allowed me into their lives to provide them the help they were seeking. If I failed in accomplishing these goals, I will at least have better tools in dealing with my guilt. If I have succeeded, then mission accomplished.

Though each client story is based on true experience, the names, sequence of events, and details have been changed to protect the privacy of the individual. Details and dialog have been both condensed and embellished for enhanced readability.

My First Client Ever

The meeting of two personalities is like the contact of two chemical substances: If there is any reaction, they are transformed. —Carl Jung

From time to time, I engage in a practice that many of my colleagues do as well—or at least should do—that is to reflect on the first client that I ever saw. These first interactions are transformative and very memorable.

Our first clients are usually the ones we saw under supervision during our practical training. When I met my first client I was a practicum student at a clinic in the South Florida area.

Ania was a twenty-one-year-old student at a local university who was referred to our counseling center. I was a novice psychology student who was tasked with helping this young woman figure out her life's issues. My upbringing in the sheltered environment of an Orthodox Jew did not provide me with many opportunities to meet with women in a meaningful way (other than with my female relatives and my wife, who was the first and last person I ever dated). I was a little nervous going into the session, although outsiders would not have been able to tell. I was given very little information about my first client except that she was a student having relationship issues.

My supervisor was a wonderful professor and mentor. Dr. Carol Rodriguez was probably the most compassionate woman I had ever met, and she cared deeply about the lives of her students.

Because I would be discussing all of my cases with Dr. Rodriguez, I was told to make it clear to my clients that I was a student clinician and that I would be reviewing what we talked about with my supervisor.

Prior to my attending graduate school, I had attended a religious school and focused on religious education. Sex was not something we talked about, and so I was caught off guard when Ania began to describe her relationship issues and sex life in graphic detail to me during our first session. (That evening I spent ten minutes in front of my mirror just practicing saying the word *sex* until I felt comfortable with it!)

As I quickly learned, Ania's sex life was not the main issue that Ania came in to discuss, but it was her way of first talking about something that she certainly felt comfortable with—although it made me squirm. Ania continued to discuss how she met her boyfriend, who was significantly older. She seemed to always seek out older men who would end up terminating the relationship, leaving Ania sad and miserable for weeks at a time. She had been taking anti-depressants but was self-medicating, not following the directions from her psychiatrist. Some days she would take her Prozac and other days, and sometimes weeks, she would purposely not take her medication. I learned over the years that there are many people who treat psychiatric medications like antibiotics. When they start feeling better they decide on their own to stop taking them rather than staying the prescribed course. I made a mental note to discuss Ania's medication noncompliance with Dr. Rodriguez.

It turns out that Ania was a very articulate and motivated client. We met weekly. She was always on time and well-dressed. She seemed to look forward to our sessions and felt she was gaining insight, although I felt I was just learning. Our sessions focused on her absent father as the possible reason why she became involved with older men, and we discussed how it was possible to have a platonic relationship with an older person without rushing into a serious one. She agreed that this was part of the problem. She always seemed to hurry into a new relationship as soon as the last one ended. She explained that this was her way of repressing her feelings about her previous lover and not having to deal with the reality of her true attachment issues.

Ania also discussed her estrangement from her mother, who still lived in Hungary. Ania loved to explore, both literally and intellectually. She loved to travel and meet new people, and she also loved to read works of philosophers. Her motivation to explore led to much of her own self-developed insight—which made my job much easier. I learned the art of therapeutic silence and used it frequently with Ania. She executed each therapeutic transaction, the basic give and take between therapist and client, with remarkable precision and insight. We both shared an interest in philosophy and our discussions often led to an understanding of the deeper meanings behind love and attachment. She was well-versed in the works of Nietzsche, Kant, and Spinoza, philosophers of whom I had only a rudimentary knowledge. I quickly read up on their works, which helped foster my understanding of some of Ania's philosophical quips.

Midway into therapy, I explored with Ania her medication noncompliance issues. She admitted that she was still not taking her Prozac on a regular basis. Her reasoning was that she wanted to be more fully in control, as opposed to having chemicals regulate her serotonin levels. I understood her rationale and mentioned to her that we would revisit the issue in a couple of weeks.

During our seventh session together, Ania came up with another revelation. She asked me how I thought she was doing in therapy. I realized that this was a question that I was supposed to be asking and not the reverse. (I would think about that and discuss it with Dr. Rodriguez during my next supervisory session.) I asked her why she was asking that question at this stage of therapy.

Her response led to my first experience with transference, where the client projects their feelings onto their therapist. Freud and others discuss transference at great length and explain that it cannot be avoided. There is not much we can do but address it when it occurs. It was about to occur with Ania.

"You see, Jonathan. I want to share something that I have been meaning to share with you but was not comfortable discussing with you until now. As you know, I am from Hungary, and you are American and also a religious Jew."

I nodded, trying to figure out where she was going with this.

"You are also around the same age as I, and I was wondering when we first met whether this would ever work out for me. I was quite surprised after our first session by how comfortable I was opening up to you about deeply personal issues. My mother never had a favorable impression of Jews, and she tried to infuse her hateful beliefs into her children. She was never successful with me as I was more a free thinker. My roommate and best friend are both Jews. I thought that you would be more judgmental of me, being that you are Jewish, but you were kind and thoughtful."

I was truly touched by her words and sentiments.

"But the main point," she continued, "was that you and I are about the same age. As we have discussed, I typically seek out older men as partners, perhaps because of my absent father. My sessions with you have made me reflect more on these choices and have given me the courage to think about dating men closer to my age. I have also enjoyed the fact that you appreciate philosophy as much as I do."

We remained silent as I digested Ania's transference.

Ania was looking at me and projecting positive feelings, which may have stemmed from her mother's negative attitude toward Jews or, more likely, from the fact that she had an absent father. I was filling a void for Ania.

"Ania, I want you to know how impressed I am with your level of insight. As I told you before we began, I am a student, and although I have some book knowledge, my therapy knowledge is limited. What I do know is that you have worked hard and that has made my job easier and, frankly, quite rewarding as a new therapist. The fact that we are of similar age might have been beneficial to you. Also, your nonjudgmental and open-minded approach to me and our sessions might have played a role in our progress together."

Ania smiled. Our time was just about up.

Our remaining sessions focused more on her relationship with her mother and accepting her past instead of ruminating about it.

By the time we had concluded our twelfth session, the semester was over, and I informed Ania that this would be our last session together. She thanked me for my help and told me that I was an excellent therapist.

I felt pretty good, and Dr. Rodriguez praised me as well, on a job well done. I reflect back on this first client at times. Just writing this story was very therapeutic and beneficial to me. I realize how far I have come in my understanding of the human condition. I also continue to agree with Freud that transference cannot and should not be avoided. It should be discussed and analyzed as it helps the process along and sifts out any interference that might be caused by projected feelings onto the therapist. I also came to realize that the case of Ania was somewhat of a teaser. Not all cases would have such happy endings.

WALK THE WALK AND TALK THE TALK

Man never made any material as resilient
as the human spirit. —Bern Williams

I am a "whatever works" kind of therapist. Remaining within the confines of an office setting can be restrictive and intimidating at the same time. Clients often feel more comfortable in alternate settings until they have developed a positive rapport with their therapist. In working with teens, this is especially true. Developing a relationship with a teenager is a daunting task for parents.

Early in my career, I would often find myself working with a teen with whom the parent or parents could not relate. Robbie was one such teen.

Robbie was sixteen years old and had been in and out of schools, mostly due to his frequent acting-out behaviors. Therapy and Robbie were like two cars on a collision course. I was the sixth therapist he would be seeing in his short life.

Since most teens are forced into therapy, the resistance is the first barrier to get through. His mother had threatened Robbie that if he did not go back to therapy, he would have to find somewhere else to live. Robbie had heard this empty threat before and challenged his mother. His father was mostly absent, having given up on Robbie many years earlier. Both parents worked full time. Mom worked as a nurse in the PICU and Dad owned his own bookselling business.

Robbie's mom called to speak with me before scheduling the appointment to see whether I would have any chance in connecting with him. She said that he is "oppositional defiant" and disrespects every authority figure that he's ever met. She liked the fact that I was relatively young compared to Robbie's past therapists. She joked that she thought the previous therapists had quit their professions because of Robbie. She said the biggest problem would be getting him to come to my Miami Beach office. I asked her where he liked to hang out. He loved the Miami Beach Boardwalk, so I suggested the Boardwalk would be a good place to start. She said that Robbie really just needed someone to talk to and connect with. I explained that I would not be Robbie's therapist at this stage unless he wanted me to serve in that role, in which case he would have to meet me at my office and make it a formal therapeutic relationship.

I suggested that I call Robbie myself. She liked the idea and gave me the number where he could be reached. She warned me that he typically hung out with other drug users who had an apartment on Collins Avenue.

I called Robbie and a croaky-voiced young man answered the phone. I introduced myself to Robbie by saying that his mother wanted me to meet with him. He asked whether I was another therapist. I said that I was and that I wanted to meet him on the Boardwalk. I quickly added, "But I don't want you to agree to meet me yet. Give it some time, think it over and then call me with your decision."

This is a tactic that I have employed numerous times when working with troubled or unconventional teens. Teens are naturally oppositional. This "oppositionality" is cultivated over many years of hearing parents and teachers say *no* too often. Learning to work with their oppositionality and giving them space and power is an art that I have mastered over the years. It's a shame that more parents don't learn this in parenting school—if it only existed! (But then again, if they did know these tactics, I would have far fewer clients.)

The next day, Robbie called and asked, "Did you say that you would meet me at the Boardwalk?"

"Yes," I replied. He said that was cool and told me what time worked best for him. I shuffled around my schedule and told him that would be fine.

There is something about walking near an ocean that is very therapeutic and gets people to open up about things they ordinarily would not discuss in the sterile conditions of a therapy office. I walked up to the meeting place that we'd mutually agreed upon and instantly spotted Robbie.

He seemed rather short for a sixteen-year-old. He had shoulder-length, dark, curly hair and acne scars. Perhaps he had a delayed growth spurt and would get taller eventually. I wondered about his level of self-consciousness and decided that I would leave if for a later discussion if he agreed to work with me.

Oftentimes adolescents are self-conscious about their appearance. A friend of mind used a "truism" to elucidate this developmental phenomenon. He said that until age twenty, people are very self-conscious about their appearance. One pimple on their face will cause them to remain in the bathroom for extended lengths of time even though the pimple is barely noticeable. At around age twenty, we decide that we don't care what other people think. Let them think what they want. Somewhere at around age forty, we come to the stark realization that no one was ever paying that much attention to what we looked like. We are all essentially self-centered.

As I introduced myself to him, he was looking around nervously. "Is this not a good place to meet?" I asked. "No, it's fine. I just was looking for my friend."

"Will your friend be joining us today?" I asked.

"No," he replied. "She just wanted to make sure I wasn't meeting some kind of weirdo." Spotting her from a distance, he waved her off. "I guess I passed the weirdo test," I chided. Robbie snickered and began coughing. He reeked of cigarette smoke, something that I have always had a strong aversion to. I decided to let him know up front. "Robbie, I just want to ask you a favor before we start. You see, I am somewhat allergic to cigarette smoke, and if you could try not to smoke while we talk, then I will remain conscious longer." He laughed again. "Fine," he said, flicking his cigarette into the bushes.

"What are we going to talk about?" Robbie asked, looking for a starting point.

"Anything you want. Obviously, I am only here because your mom wanted me to meet with you. I understand that you did not have such great experiences with your previous therapists."

"Yeah. They all sucked. Especially when they kept insisting that we all meet together. But they never met me at the Boardwalk. Is this your office?" he joked.

"Today it is," I responded. "But I really just want to spend my time getting to know you a little better. Your mom said that you liked to hang out here."

"Yeah, it helps me clear my head," he said staring off across the beautiful Atlantic.

"Me too. . . . I see you were listening to music before I got here. What music do you like?"

He rattled off several bands. I was familiar with a few, but about the others I was admittedly clueless. "Do you play an instrument too?" I asked. "Guitar," he said. "Love the guitar."

"Can I listen to one of the songs?" He handed me the headphones and played me one of his favorites, which happened to be one that I knew. We continued our walk and Robbie talked about many things, from music and his friends to the schools he previously attended. He proved to be a pretty good conversationalist for a teen and I commended him on this. "Did you ever think of becoming a therapist?" I asked jokingly.

"I already am," he responded. "For some reason everyone comes to me with their problems. I really don't know what I am doing, but I just listen. It makes my problems seem so small when I hear some of theirs. Like one friend is always telling me that he is going to kill himself. I'm kind of worried about him. His girlfriend just dumped him, and he sits around crying all day. I told him that he needs to get some serious help, but he refuses. He's seriously messed up. Maybe I should take him here to the beach and see whether he'll open up better."

Robbie and I continued discussing issues that he had with certain friends. As it was getting close to my next appointment, I told him that it had been really nice to meet him and wished him luck with his friends.

As I was walking down the steps of the boardwalk toward my car, he called out to me, "When are we meeting again?" I said, "Give me a call and we can schedule another appointment if you want."

A day later, Robbie's mother called to ask whether I'd met with Robbie. I told her we had and that he wished to schedule another session. Impressed, she asked, "How did you make that happen?" I explained to her that Robbie is very used to being told what to do, and so far that tactic from his teachers and his parents has not gotten very far with him. Robbie likes to do things on his own terms. I let him take the lead. I then told Robbie's mom that I would like to make it formal therapy because I would not always be able to go to the Boardwalk. She came in the next day and signed the forms, and I implored her not to ask Robbie about anything he talks about in therapy or else it would not work. She agreed, and I told her that I would be telling Robbie that, with the usual exceptions, I would not discuss anything we talk about with his parents.

Robbie was out of school during the weeks we met and spent most of his days hanging out with friends, smoking pot and playing guitar. His friends, for the most part, came from families lacking any positive role models.

For our first formal sit-down therapy session, Robbie had put on a pair of clean jeans. I decided not to comment on it at the time. He asked me questions about the qualifications of a therapist and how long it takes to get through school to become one. I asked him why he was so interested. He said that no adult had ever suggested that he would be good at anything until I mentioned the therapist idea. He thought it sounded cool.

"What about finishing high school first?" I asked.

"I was thinking about that, and I decided that instead of going back to high school I would just get my GED and apply to college."

"Sounds like you have been doing a lot of thinking," I reframed.

"As I told you, I do my best thinking near the ocean. I am seeing the path that my friends are taking, and it does not look like a path I want to continue taking."

"What about your parents?" I asked.

"I don't know. We don't get along, and they want me to be in a regular high school just like everyone else. They won't listen to the idea of me getting my GED. They think you can't get into any decent college with a GED."

"Would it be okay if I try to talk to them about it? Perhaps I can have an influence on them. They seem to trust me so far," I said.

"Good luck," was Robbie's response.

We continued to talk about music, which seemed to be a true passion of his. I was very impressed with his ability to articulate himself. He then took out a folded piece of paper from his jeans' pocket that contained the lyrics of a song he had just written. After reading the lyrics, I said, "This is really impressive stuff, Robbie!"

"You really like it?" he asked, this time sounding more like a child seeking approval.

"Yeah," I responded. "Maybe fewer cuss words, but otherwise there is a great message in those lyrics." I believe that Robbie saw that I was genuinely interested in music, which is very true, and our connection strengthened. Now I had to work on his parents.

Robbie's parents were open to the idea of meeting with me. They asked whether Robbie would be there as well. I told them he wouldn't be this time. When his parents arrived, they were not the type of parents I had anticipated, which is not unusual. Although therapists can be decent forecasters of character, we also make mistakes and flawed attributions. It seemed as though Robbie's father wanted to make a good first impression. He presented as a very self-confident, well-dressed man with tremendous concern for his son's well-being. This seemed very different from the depiction that Robbie and his mom had given about the dad being an absent parent. He began the session by thanking me profusely for taking Robbie on as a client and went on to admit that he has made many mistakes in his parenting of Robbie.

His mother, on the other hand, had seemed far more pessimistic as she reminded her husband and me of all the fruitless efforts of past interventions. His father was unnerved and pressed on that it was he, as the father, who needed to make changes in his life to connect with Robbie.

Mother seemed baffled by her husband's latest epiphany. I was not sure what to make of the give and take. Was Robbie's father just putting on a show or was he for real? I gave him the benefit of the doubt based on Mom's reaction and validated him.

"I am very impressed by your willingness to make changes in your parenting of Robbie. It is not very common that I find parents who are amenable to new approaches. I commend you both for that." I intentionally included the mother in this statement in order to keep them both present for the process.

I explained to them that Robbie and I had connected very well and that this would be a golden opportunity for them to make changes that would impact Robbie's future. I suggested that a good first step would be for Robbie and his dad to spend some quality time together. Maybe he could take a day off and offer to take Robbie to a guitar shop, but he should let Robbie choose the time and day to go. Since Dad owned his own business, he was able to be flexible with his schedule. To help, I even gave him a script of what to say to Robbie. He seemed pleased with the idea.

Then I decided that it would be a good time to bring up the GED. I informed them that Robbie had expressed an interest in getting his GED because school was not working out for him. His mother immediately objected, saying that he would get nowhere with a GED. I responded that I have had many clients who were able to move on without an official high school diploma. His father seemed fine with the idea and turned to his wife and said, "I think the guy is right. We should just be happy that he is connecting well with someone and is open to getting his GED. We are not expecting Robbie to go to Harvard, and he doesn't need to."

I agreed and reiterated that Robbie was entering a better place and giving him more latitude to do things that are positive would be the right direction to take as parents. I had no reservations about Robbie's ability to pass his GED but still I recommended a tutor to help him along. Dad was already on board, but Mom was less optimistic.

I asked her, "What was your hope for Robbie?" At this point she began to emote. She acknowledged that Robbie was very bright and as a kid he'd read a lot and done well in school. When he began to hang out with a "different" crowd, things began to go downhill quickly. With his new "goth" friends, he began to dress differently and listened to music that she could never appreciate.

This is a topic that I was very familiar with. I told her that I once gave a speech on how to ensure a distant relationship with your teenager. Just do the following three things: criticize their friends, their music, and their clothes. These are the three most important things to teens at this stage of a child's development. Taking those three things away from them or, worse yet, criticizing them creates distance. I have found this to be true time and time again, no matter what your generation.

She looked up and said, "I guess I am guilty of all three." I quickly responded that it is too early in the process to give up and assured her that this is the opportune time to make amends. We talked about the guilt process and my theory of productive guilt. She was ready to take the journey from "guilt ridden" to "guilt riddance."

Robbie's parents left the session, and I was hopeful that they would be able to remain calm and resolute in their ability to make those changes.

Robbie called me to make another appointment. When he walked in the door, I saw a different child. Robbie was dressed in a two-piece suit and his hair was neatly cropped. I jokingly asked, "Are you going on a date?"

"No," he replied. "I have an interview at a law firm to do some shadowing."

"I didn't know you were interested in law," I said curiously.

"I didn't know either. I still don't know, but my dad took me out on Sunday to look for guitars and we actually had a good time. At the guitar shop, I met a lawyer who was looking for someone to do some filing over the summer, and he said he would be willing to meet with me."

"What about taking your GED?"

"Well, I don't know what you said to my parents, but they are acting very different toward me. It's weird. Did you hypnotize them or something?" We both laughed. "Anyway, they said it would be fine for me to take the GED, and they were happy that I would get to shadow this lawyer."

Robbie and I continued to work together and eventually we met together as a family. Robbie and his parents looked very comfortable with each other. His mother changed her nursing schedule so that she could be around more for Robbie. With Robbie in the waiting room, she said to me with tears in her eyes, "Do you know that every night before he goes to bed now, he gives me a hug and tells me that he loves me?"

I smiled, holding back my own tears and said, "Keep up the great work. He is a terrific kid!"

"Yes, he is," she replied "and I can't thank you enough for getting me to realize that."

Irvin Yalom, in his book *The Gift of Therapy*, asserts that therapy has become too restrictive and does not allow therapists to work effectively out of fear that an out-of-the-box approach, such as making home visits, would come back to haunt the therapist. I agree with him. I believe we have created an environment where therapists cannot be human. They must act robotic and limit what they do to the confines of a fifty-minute hour. If we were to take a journey back in time, most physicians, my grandfather included, would make home visits as a routine part of their practice.

Flexibility in therapy is not widely practiced anymore. However, even within the boundaries that many therapists are restricted to, we still can find some flexibility in how we deal with issues. We could possibly be doing harm to our clients with the cold, clinical approach we are being taught to use.

Robbie would have never engaged in therapeutic services on his own or at the direction of his parents. It does not take a seasoned therapist to recognize the natural resistance of an adolescent. However, the mature therapist recognizes that he must establish a rapport with the client, however unconventional that method might be.

I wonder where Robbie would be now if we had not met initially at the Boardwalk.

What's That Fool Thing on Your Head?

Success seems to be largely a matter of hanging on when others have let go. —William Feather

As a yarmulke-wearing mental health professional in an inner-city school district, it would suffice to say that I stood out like a sore thumb. I first began working with inner-city kids in January of 2000 after completing an internship at what was then known as Baywood Island Psychiatric Hospital.

Focusing primarily on the psychological needs of geriatric patients, the internship didn't prepare me for counseling youth. A colleague of mine described the catatonic hospital patients as sitting in "God's waiting room," also known as South Florida—a far cry from West Baltimore.

My first assignment in the city schools found me at Fillmore Middle School, a large, imposing red brick building near

Johns Hopkins Hospital. It was in need of serious renovation. The foul air in the building was unbearable at times; the windows could not be opened because they were barred shut and had window AC units in them—that only made the space hotter instead of cooler. I had a choice of two possible offices to use as a counseling room, neither of which afforded me any privacy or breathable air. Choice A was a small, mold-infested room on the ground level shared by four other employees, and Choice B was a rat-infested room on the top floor with the rowdy sixth graders. I chose mold over rats. (A little brain damage from mold toxins shouldn't be much of a problem, I decided).

The problem was that most of the students I counseled were on the top floor, which meant schlepping up a few flights of stairs several times a day because there were, of course, no working elevators. The school social worker seeing me sweating profusely as I made the climb simply said, "You'll get used to it."

"Thanks," I replied, glad I'd been generous that morning with Right Guard. This was my first day at the school and first time working with inner-city students.

I vividly remember my first meeting with Henry. Henry was a tall, lanky sixth-grader who seemed to be the class ringleader. He was charged with getting as many adults as possible to quit under his watch. As an Orthodox Jew with a yarmulka on my head, I knew the question would come sooner or later, so I used an old trick that my friend David had taught me. Henry saw me walking down the hall and screamed out, "Yo!"

By that time the crowd had grown to about a dozen to see the new kid on the block—me! Again he said, "Yo!"

I turned around and asked, "Are you talking to me?" He continued, "Wha's dat foo' thing on yo' head?"

Pretending I did not understand him correctly, I again asked, "What did you say?"

"Wha's dat foo' thing on yo' head?" Henry clarified.

This time, acting nervous, I asked, "What thing on my head?" Pointing to my head, he said, "That black thing."

Again I asked in my nervous voice, "What black thing?"

Henry persisted. By this time almost the entire sixth grade had surrounded me like I was some street performer in front of a very captive audience. Henry said, "There is a black thing on your head."

On cue, I reached up and swatted the black thing (my yarmulke) off my head and screamed, "THERE'S A BLACK THING ON MY HEAD! GET IT OFF ME!"

The sixth-graders and Henry all had a good laugh, and then Henry said, "You must be the new school psychologist. You're pretty damn funny!"

I was happy with my performance—it helped break the ice. I thanked him, took a bow, and went down to the mold-infested office. I looked around and saw people swamped with paperwork, which I soon learned were the lengthy Individualized Educational Plans known as IEPs.

Henry eventually became my first "client" at the school. In the inner city, an outsider who happens to be a mental health provider is likely to have difficulty engaging a troubled child in counseling. Therefore, I had to use as many tricks as possible to get Henry to fulfill the requirements of his IEP, which required he come see the "funny Jewish guy" once a week.

When I first called Henry down to my office, he refused to come. "I ain't goin' with you and I ain't talkin' to you!" I bargained: "Okay. I'll make you a deal. Meet me in the gym. If you beat me in a one-on-one, you don't have to ever talk to me again. If you lose, we meet weekly and try to resolve your unconscious inner conflicts." Henry looked confused but laughed and said plainly, "You can't play ball."

Little did Henry know, but I had been a pretty good basketball player in my day. Although Henry was a sixth-grader, he had two inches on me at six feet. I smiled back and said, "You may be right. Are you game?"

Henry's comrades joined Henry in the gym to watch a match as if it were Kobe Bryant versus Steph Curry. When it was 9–1 in my favor, Henry's comrades were confused. "Come on Henry. You can't let that old guy beat you." The final score was Dr. Lasson, 11, Henry 2. Defeated but with resolve, Henry said, "Not bad for an old white dude." We had hit it off. Henry was now my weekly client.

Henry was a bright young man who was not achieving academically and had a few run-ins with law enforcement. I would soon learn that run-ins with law enforcement were somewhat commonplace, even for sixth-graders in the inner city. Tensions between the police and the black community existed long before the Freddie Gray riots of 2015. Henry did not like the police and had issues with authority, in general.

There were obvious reasons for his distrust, which we would explore in counseling sessions.

According to the psychological evaluation conducted by the previous school psychologist, Henry carried multiple diagnoses of oppositional defiant disorder, attention deficit hyperactivity disorder, predominantly hyperactive type, and learning disorder, NOS (not otherwise specified). I have always questioned the premature diagnosing of school children and the labeling that would follow them for years. Henry was supposedly taking Ritalin, but his guardian stated that he was noncompliant, which was an all too common problem with middle-school students.

Finding a place to meet Henry was another problem. He did not like meeting me in the mold room because he did not get along with some of the authority figures in that office, namely the principal. He also did not like the rat room because he did not want his peers to see that he was coming to meet with me. So we agreed to meet after his fourth period in the gym, and then he could go straight to lunch. This arrangement worked out very well. At times we talked and at other times we practiced layups and three-point shots. Henry's basketball skills improved, as did his academics. This was partially due to bribes from the idealistic school psychologist whose sole mission was to save Henry from ending up on the streets—or worse. Nothing scared me more than having to attend the funeral of a child I worked with. I never thought it would happen.

Unfortunately, it did. Not with Henry, but with others.

Henry was a different story. Henry, unlike most of my family members, actually found me to be pretty funny. He laughed at my jokes and worked hard to come up with his own. We talked about his family, from whom he was pretty much estranged. He had been in and out of foster care. He did not disclose a history of abuse, but it was in his records. I decided not to address those issues so early in our relationship. I had developed a nice rapport with Henry and did not want to disrupt the connection that I worked so hard to establish. After several weeks, I realized what needed to happen in order to give Henry a shot at making it out of middle school without too much damage: I had to get him out of the city.

A few weeks after meeting Henry, a call came from the school social worker saying that Henry had been arrested for shoplifting. She wanted me to address the issue with Henry, along with his general defiance toward the police, and any authority figures, for that matter. I was surprised that Henry continued to have these issues with the law, but he had already developed a reputation in the neighborhood as a trouble-maker. I asked the social worker about his family.

She sighed and said, "There is no family." I had known this already from Henry, but I wanted more information from an adult who knew Henry's history. I said, "He has to have some-one in his life who would be willing to mentor him." She told me that Henry did have an aunt and uncle who lived in At-lanta, but they did not want to have anything to do with Henry or his family.

Henry's father had been killed when Henry was three and his mother was incarcerated for drugs and prostitution. The social worker, anticipating my next question, said, "And yes, Dr. Lasson, I already tried calling them." I said, "Please let me try." Reluctantly, she gave me their number. I put it away for later because I had to attend to another crisis: apparently the speech pathologist was having a panic attack because there was a cockroach the size of an adult iguana sitting on top of a report she had just typed up.

During my lunch break, I walked up to Johns Hopkins Hospital to get a coffee and clear my mind of the school—and the mold. I took out the piece of paper with the number of Henry's aunt and uncle and called. I identified myself to them; they seemed surprised by the call. I explained to them that Henry was a bright child (I knew this from his IQ testing). I told them how well he had been responding to working with me and my approach.

I had learned another tactic over the years: when you want something, it's best not to make a formal request but rather make a connection. I asked them if I could update them on Henry's progress from time to time. They seemed okay with the idea. They had only met Henry when he was less than three years old and would not recognize this six-foot sixth-grader if they bumped into him. I left them my number and told them that they could call me at any time if they felt there was anything to share that would help me in working with Henry.

The following day I met with Henry and asked him about his relatives in Atlanta. He didn't remember them but had heard they were rich. He sighed and looked down. I remained quiet. He finally looked up at me and asked, "You mad at me,

Doc?" I asked him why he would think that, and he reminded me about the shoplifting arrest. I explained to him that I was not upset with him and that people make mistakes all the time. We then had a very intellectual conversation about why people steal. Henry understood that he was trying to replace the many losses in his life with tangible items. This was not the first time he had shoplifted, he explained, just the first time he was caught. Things had clicked well between Henry and me. He was no longer embarrassed to be seen with me and, in fact, his friends were jealous that he got free sandwiches from the new psychologist. Some of his friends asked him how they could get an IEP . . . and a sandwich.

It seemed that Henry still felt as though he had let me down, so I suggested we shoot some hoops. Henry was noticeably more quiet than usual. After shooting for a while, we sat on the bench and Henry turned to me and said, "Thank you, Doc."

There are some precious moments where mental health professionals feel like they are making a difference. They do not happen very often when working with an impoverished population of good kids who are caught up within a negative and hostile environment. It takes lots of time and thinking out of the box just to build that trusting relationship that will help make the connection last.

Over the next few weeks, Henry's demeanor and attitude toward me, his teachers, and his academics began to change. His grades began to improve and there were fewer acting-out incidents reported. Even the principal, who had Henry on his "one foot out the door" list, noted the change. I felt proud that

I had maintained this connection with a promising young man who had so much to offer if his energies were channeled in the right direction.

I decided to look at his file a little more carefully. Combing through his records, something else stood out about Henry. When he was in fourth grade, his IEP stated that he was visually impaired and required glasses. I never noticed Henry wearing glasses and highly doubted that he wore contacts. I asked him about it during the next session. He said that he does have trouble seeing the board, but he did not want to wear glasses. I contacted his guardian who informed me that she once got Henry a pair but he broke them. I discussed this with Henry. He said he didn't really break them but had thrown them away because he did not want to be picked on by his classmates. I learned that students in the inner-city schools do not like to wear glasses out of a fear of looking smart. If you look smart, then you do not fit in with the cool group. Henry wanted to fit in. His guardian said that she couldn't afford to buy him another pair, and why should she if he was going to break them anyway. I spoke to the school social worker. The next week Henry had a new pair of glasses, courtesy of medical assistance.

We were almost at the end of the school year and Henry continued to improve. He was now at the top of the class in reading and mathematics, and his IEP would change so that he would not be in a self-contained class for the following year. Now was my chance. I called his relatives in Atlanta. I explained to them that Henry would only survive given a change in his environment. I shared with them his progress and that he had been incident-free for more than four months.

I asked them to think about the idea of taking him in on a trial basis and get back to me with their decision.

Three weeks later, I received a call from his aunt. She was a paralegal and articulated her concerns with the mannerisms of a woman who walked the courtroom halls many a time. She stated that she would draw up stipulations that would enable Henry to live with her family in Atlanta. She said that after discussing it with her husband, they agreed to take him into their home and send him to the same private school that their son had been attending. Henry's uncle was on the school board and would be able to enroll Henry without much effort. I was elated and shared the news with Henry. He was happy but also worried about the adjustment. We talked about it for a while and I explained the stipulation until I felt comfortable Henry understood that he would have to come back if things didn't work out or he messed up.

Henry got to a place where he was in agreement with the idea of moving and starting anew. He asked if he would have to continue seeing a therapist in Atlanta. I said it would be a good idea to have someone to talk to because this would be a new adjustment for him. He was concerned that we would lose our connection. I assured him that I would stay in touch. He gave me a knuckle high five and a "Thank you, Doc." And so began my nearly fourteen-year career working with inner-city children.

Reflecting back almost sixteen years later, I am reminded of the famous starfish story that was told to me when I first entered the field. It is about a boy who would sit on the beach picking up starfish that had washed ashore and throw them back in the ocean so they would not die. An older man, after watching the little boy do this for a while, asked him why he was throwing the starfish back when it would hardly make a difference given the number that were being washed up on the shore. The little boy picked up another starfish and threw it out to the ocean and said to the old man, "I made a difference for that one."

When working with a population with such a high recidivism rate, you might feel like you are not making a dent or even a miniscule difference in the lives of the kids you serve. We have to focus on that starfish that we did help. Henry was my first starfish.

THERAPY OR
CONFESSION

Strive not to be of success,
but rather to be of value. —Albert Einstein

Therapists hear lots of stories. Therapists also hear lots of confessions. We are not pastoral counselors, although we have the ability to counsel. Often I wonder whether my function as a therapist is to serve as one who receives confessions as a method of easing a deep psychological scar. Indeed, at the height of my practice, I had many clients who specifically requested a "religious-minded" therapist. To many, the confluence of therapy and religion is not possible, and they shy away from discussing faith-based matters in therapy.

Many people in the mental health field who are not religious will, at times, have difficulty treating a religious client. Especially if they've had a negative experience with religion or with a devout person. Therefore, religious people often tend to choose religious therapists. For example, a rabbi came to see me about an issue he was having with his teenage daughter. He was relieved to learn that I was an Orthodox Jew. He went on to explain that the last therapist that his daughter had seen suggested to her that many of her issues stemmed from living a religious lifestyle and that she was old enough to decide her own level of spiritual observance. Thankfully, the majority of therapists I know would never make such a suggestion as it is counter-intuitive to suggest to a fifteen-year-old girl who already has issues with authority that she rebel against her faith, which, in her mind, was just another authority figure.

Jerome, a sixty-year-old man from Jamaica, came from a mostly stable, religious-minded home. His parents were ardent churchgoers, and he had enjoyed many aspects of spiritual life, especially the music. His family loved to sing, and he was an excellent pianist. He married an equally religious young lady and, to outsiders, they led an ideal life. In the clinic where I was working in Miami, most of the religious clients were referred to me, and Jerome specifically chose to see me for this reason.

Jerome presented as an articulate, mild-mannered man who appeared his stated age. He was quite tall, well over six feet, with an air of confidence that I did not quite expect based on the general description I was given by the secretary who conducted the phone intake. She had said he seemed very nervous on the phone. He offered a firm handshake and took a seat on the couch. He looked around the room, as if taking in his environment, and asked, "So this is it?"

"What do you mean?" I asked.

"I have never been to therapy before, and I guess I was expecting something different."

"Well, we have not even started. What exactly were you expecting?"

"A different decor for one," he replied with a hearty laugh. I was struck right away by Jerome's beautiful baritone voice, and it was evident that either he had received musical training or at least had natural talent.

I smiled. "What else?"

"I thought the room would be larger. This seems more like a room for a confessional?"

"Does this room make you uncomfortable?" I asked.

"No. It's just that I am used to confession rooms, as a churchgoing man. I was not quite expecting such an intimate-looking room."

"Did you come here to make a confession?"

"In a sense, yes. But I guess I also came for some deeper understanding."

"What are you trying to understand?"

At this point Jerome shifted in his seat. On the intake form, the limited information stated that Jerome was coming in due to intense anxiety and difficulty sleeping. Until this point I saw a very confident, articulate gentleman. The shifting indicated to me that there was something causing him anxiety. Also, the line he dropped about a confession led me to make the "clever" assumption that he had a secret. (They train us to pick up on stuff like that.)

Our job as therapists is to create the best possible environment for our clients to feel safe and secure that what they share is confidential.

"Doc, I am embarrassed to talk about this. I have never told this to anyone." My silence encouraged him to continue. "I don't want you to judge me by what I am about to share with you."

I assured him that he would not be judged. "Jerome, I know this must be difficult and something has been weighing on your mind for a long time. I want to encourage you to speak openly and freely about whatever is bothering you."

He looked up, down, and all around the room and gave a heavy sigh. "I can't believe I am telling you this. I am basically leading a double life." More silence. "My wife has no clue, but I meet with other men for sex. It is just for sex and nothing else. I am not looking for romance, but I feel a warm connection when I am with other men. And don't worry. It is with older men like me, who are not part of the church. I meet most of them online."

Jerome seemed to have been looking for an expression of intense shock from me. I remained poker-faced and encouraged him to continue.

"My wife would never understand this. We have a great relationship, outside of sex. We enjoy going to concerts and eating Chinese. We also both love walking on the boardwalk, which we do every Sunday after church."

This was not the first religious person or a member of the clergy, for that matter, who outed himself or herself to me.

"Are you surprised, Dr. Lasson? Because if you are, you are not showing it."

"Jerome, I have only known you for about fifteen minutes. People, especially religious people, come to me all the time feeling guilty about things that they have thought about doing or have done, which are often sexual in nature. I want to remind you that you are not here for judgment. I am not here to receive a confession. We are both here to get a better understanding of your anxiety and to better help you deal with your feelings of guilt."

Jerome eased up and became more comfortable. "This is somewhat of a relief to me. As I told you, I have never shared this with anyone. I see that you wear a yarmulke on your head. You must be a man of the book as well."

I nodded.

"So how do you know that we are not all going to hell? We all sin." Jerome wondered aloud.

I was not about to get into a philosophical or theological discussion with Jerome about the virtues that gain you entry into heaven or hell. Anyway, I am not an expert in that area. I did decide to challenge his thoughts to some extent: "Have you met sinners before?"

"Indeed. People confess to me all the time," he offered.

"Jerome, what would you say is one of your most admirable traits?"

"I overheard my wife talking to her friend about me once: 'I've never heard Jerome raise his voice or say a negative thing about anyone.' I guess that is somewhat admirable."

"Somewhat?" I asked encouraging elaboration and insight.

"I guess you are saying that I have a pretty admirable trait if I do not speak slander."

"Correct!" I said enthusiastically. "How does that make you feel to hear that?"

"I guess it makes me feel pretty good. But what about my sins?"

"Jerome, do you know how God tallies up sins versus good deeds?"

"No," he responded.

"Well, that makes two of us." Jerome and I both laughed. "You mean three of us," Jerome said pointing upward. We laughed again.

"Let's imagine that you are having a conversation with God about your sins versus your good deeds. How do you think it would go?"

"I would assume that I would start with what I am feeling most guilty about."

"And let's say that God says to you, 'Jerome, the fact that you never speak slander about me is more covetous to me than any possible perceived sin that you want to admit to me'," I proposed in my most Godly sounding voice.

"I guess I will not know how to respond until I get there."

"Correct again. Where do you think I am going with this?"

"It sounds to me like you are saying that I should be spending more mental energy focusing on my positive or more admirable traits than my 'perceived sins'."

I smiled.

"This is a lot for me to digest. I will have to give it some thought." Our hour was just about up. Jerome got up and shook my hand. "Thank you, Doc. When can we meet again?"

I recommended the following week.

When Jerome came in for the next session he was singing a tune. As a music lover, I could hear how talented this man was. I commented as he walked in, "You have a magnificent voice, Jerome." He thanked me and said, "I tend to sing more when I am feeling good."

"And why, pray tell, are you feeling so good today, Jerome?" I asked with curiosity.

He held up his fingers as if making quotations signs, "Well, my 'confession' to you last session certainly helped, and the fact that I know you are not judging me has put me at ease to a great extent."

Sensing there was more, I put out my hand as if to say . . . "And?"

"I did some reading and praying, and some more reading and praying. I realized that my prayers had been lacking something. In the past, I was praying more out of fear. Now I am praying more out of love."

The profundity of that statement gave me pause. "I will have to think about that one."

Jerome's transformation over the next few weeks was nothing short of remarkable. He was highly motivated to work on himself and stated that he had been sleeping very soundly. He told me he was enjoying his time as he nears retirement. "I will never completely retire until I expire," he joked. At our last session he said to me, "Doc, I am really look-ing forward to meeting God." Noting my concerned expres-sion, he added, "Don't worry. I will let him take me when *he* is ready."

Jerome was one of those enjoyable clients who possessed many capabilities. His ability to come to the realization that his guilt would get him nowhere fast was most helpful to him. I have worked with religious people and members of the clergy before and usually enjoy our back and forth discussions. Jerome ended up leaving his position with the church and pursuing other interests that had been dormant for years. He continued to pursue his passion for music and philosophy. He continued to lead a religious life, but on different terms.

Jerome informed me during our last session that he wanted to have a conversation with his wife and asked for advice as to what he should say to her. I provided him the names of mar-riage therapists in the area. He and his wife remained com-mitted to each other on an intellectual level. Their mutual respect for each other would carry them through the difficult time that would inevitably come once Jerome informed her about his sexual preference.

Upon reflection, I look back at Jerome and his dilemma. It took him so long to broach the subject of his sexuality with someone. Once he accomplished that, he was free of most of his anxieties. Jerome thanked me for being nonjudgmental.

I advise my clients that I am not a rabbi or a member of the clergy. I try my best to remain nonjudgmental, leaving judg-ment to higher powers. The role of receiving confessions is one I've never wanted to assume, but invariably it becomes part of the job. People will confess to the clergy, but therapy oftentimes creates a venue for a different kind of confessional, one that incorporates and facilitates insight. As therapists, we are often told not to mix religion with therapy. However, there is a reason why people choose to see a religious therapist. We must go in the direction that the river of therapy flows. If it takes us down a spiritual path, then so be it.

Narcissism and Wooden Ducks

Whoever loves becomes humble. Those who love have, so to speak, pawned a part of their narcissism. —Sigmund Freud

In my experience, one of the most difficult client populations to treat are those with narcissistic tendencies. They rarely have the capacity to empathize and cause much grief to their relatives (and therapists) Trying to get them to understand the root of their issues is usually an exercise in futility. In graduate school, I wondered why these individuals would ever seek therapy. I soon realized that they do not, for the most part, seek out professional help. Often it is a family member who demands they see a therapist. Or they get themselves into trouble, and the court orders them to come for therapy.

Simon was one such case. Simon's wife, Maria, wanted a divorce, and the only way she would consider taking him back into her life was if he went for treatment. Simon presented as a very handsome young man who seemed more concerned about wrinkling his pants than the process of therapy. After my formal introductions, which Simon did not seem at all interested in hearing, Simon nonchalantly said, "You know I'm only here because my wife is blackmailing me." This was not going to be a "Simple Simon." However, I do enjoy an occasional challenge.

Noticing my relatively young age, Simon asked me where I had gone to school. When I told him, he said he'd never heard of it. I questioned him, doing my best not to sound defensive, as to whether he typically begins conversations in this style. He responded, "I have been told that I could be abrasive at times, but that's what got me this far in life." Indeed, Simon had been successful career-wise, but his social adeptness, or lack thereof, caused many to distance themselves from Simon.

Simon worked in the real estate business and made his money buying and flipping homes in impoverished neighborhoods. Never quite satisfied with the amount of money he was making, he had a side business involving credit cards, which I never understood very well, but it sounded like a scam. He enjoyed taking advantage of vulnerable individuals and offered them promises that he could not possibly keep. He was taken to court and sued for lots of money. He hired some savvy lawyers, with the aid of his very wealthy father, who successfully helped him avoid prison time, instead paying a fee for his scandalous ways. I imagined the pain he must have caused those poor people.

While Simon was involved in the business of ripping off almost everyone he met, he had an ongoing affair with another woman. This woman would prove to be Simon's undoing. Simon was pretty good at hiding his infidelity but in this day and age, it's more and more difficult to engage in adultery without getting caught. Maria was tempted to hire a private investigator to follow him around, but she decided to do her own investigation.

One morning Simon told his wife that he would be going out of town for the next couple of days for a big business deal. She borrowed a friend's car and followed him for about twenty minutes. Simon had apparently arranged to meet his mistress at a Dunkin' Donuts and then drive out to the country for a two-day rendezvous. Maria pulled into the Dunkin' Donuts parking lot and spotted Simon escorting his mistress into his Porsche. Maria immediately phoned Simon. She saw Simon look at his phone, but he did not pick up. She redialed his number. This time he answered the phone and told her he could not speak because he was at the check-in counter at the airport and it was his turn. Maria snarled, "Since when did Dunkin' Donuts fly planes?" She then hung up, bumped his car with hers and flipped him the bird.

Simon, realizing he had been caught red-handed, attempted to make up another story about how he did not want to tell Maria his whereabouts because he needed some time away from the daily grind and that he was taking a friend to an antique store. Maria said, "Don't bother coming back home." Maria sobbed and thought about the prospects of being alone and being a single mom to their four-year-old son. She offered Simon reconciliation, provided that he attend and participate in therapy.

I think Simon only heard the "attend" part because the first session with me seemed to be a total waste of his—and my—time. He rationalized that most men had affairs and that Maria should learn to get over it. He also understood that Maria was dependent on him for financial reasons. His resistance was perplexing. I felt absolutely no connection with this man whom I was supposed to help. He put up a barrier that would rival the Great Wall of China. Unfortunately, it was true. Simon did not need Maria as much as Maria needed him. Maria had not worked in years and was left to take care of her son mostly by herself. No one ever said that therapy was a piece of cake, and this session was falling apart faster than most crumb cakes.

Drawing from my therapy tool kit, which only exists in the mind of a therapist, I attempted an intervention. Playing into his narcissism, I said to Simon, "I think I would personally benefit from seeing you for a few more sessions. I see that you have a lot to offer. You are smart and savvy and maybe you can teach me a thing or two." It was a risk. But Simon took the bait.

Smiling back at me Simon said, "I don't know you well, but I can make you into a rich man, Doc."

He then outlined a plan of how I should do therapy via Skype to some very wealthy people he knew and charge four times what I was presently charging. He also said that he knew some hotshots who worked in Hollywood and he could get me an appearance on The Jerry Springer Show. Pretending to be very impressed and excited at the same time, I said, "That sounds amazing. Let's explore those ideas next week. Thank you so much! You are brilliant." After Simon left the office I worried about what I was getting myself into.

Simon walked into the next session even better dressed than the first. He began the session by saying that if I got a fancier office in a better neighborhood, I would make more money. This seemed to be the driving force behind Simon: making loads of money. I was caught in an existential dilemma. I abhor materialistic things, although it would be nice to be able to pay for some of the basics without a struggle. I do not envy those with large homes. I would not know what to do with a fancy car. I don't pick out my own clothing because the fashion police would be all over me. (Thank goodness for my wife.) Watching Simon, I recalled the Talmudic expression, *the more possessions, the more worries.* How was I going to get Simon back on track and discuss his reason for being in therapy?

I thanked Simon for his suggestions of upgrading my office to the likes of the Waldorf Astoria and made a deal with him. "Simon, I want to continue where we left off last session and explore ideas about how to make me more successful, but I would feel much better if we attempted to work on the issues that your wife would like for you to work on."

Not expecting this, Simon said, "I already had a long talk with Maria; we reconciled."

"Oh, how did that go?"

He went on to tell me how he took her out to her favorite restaurant and told her that he is committed to therapy and begged her to reconsider. He then took off the next couple of days from "work" and wined and dined her into submission.

"So why did you come back this week?"

"Well I want to help *you*, Doc," was his reply. It's a simple business plan. Of course, Simon wanted a cut. He outlined what he envisioned as a "no-brainer" where I could do my "psychobabble stuff" online and make a mint. I was then to write a book about how I saved his marriage, he would get the royalties, and I would pursue speaking engagements with all the connections he had in Hollywood.

There comes a point in therapy where a therapist has dug a pit that is too deep to climb out of. My sessions with Simon seemed to be a prime example. There was no way that I could convince Simon that he would continue to have the same problems, so I had to find a way to bail out. I chose honesty. "Simon, your plans sound really exciting, but I truly do not have an interest in making a lot of money off people. I like to help people to the point where they become insightful and can figure out how to resolve their own problems. I find that more empowering than having a really nice BMW."

He stood up and looked at me as if I just lost out on the deal of a lifetime. He gave me his business card and told me to call him if I wanted to reconsider. I shook his hand and thanked him as he left. Ripping the business card into shreds, I sat back in my chair and smiled with a deep sense of relief.

I looked around my modest office adorned with wooden ducks. The Chinese view the mandarin duck as a symbol of love and peaceful relationships. My goal as a therapist is to bring my sense of inner peace to my clients, and the ducks remind me of what really matters to me.

I truly felt bad for Simon for not having the capacity to understand and appreciate the simple things in life. My strategy to go along with his plan to make me rich and famous did not work. However, it had a long-lasting impact for me—perhaps a therapeutic impact—by affirming my value of living a life that is true to myself. I decided to buy a two-dollar wooden duck that I had seen at a yard sale earlier that day. Now my office felt more complete.

SMALL DOSES

Failure is not falling down,
but refusing to get up. —Chinese proverb

amilies are interesting. A friend of mine likes to joke that his family puts the "fun" into dysfunction. I don't know many people who could honestly say their family is perfectly "normal," they get along all the time, always eat meals together and nobody fights. Honestly, do any of us know Brady Bunch families who sing Kumbaya together and give each other warm hugs before going to sleep? As a therapist, I certainly learn about more than my fair share of "fun" families.

Corey was a twenty-eight-year-old woman who came to me for therapy after initially requesting a female therapist. Since I was the only clinician available for the next two weeks, she reluctantly agreed to meet with me for one session. She was in a crisis, according to the secretary who conducted the phone intake, although she would not elaborate what that crisis was over the phone.

When I went to call her into my office, I noticed Corey looked quite agitated. She nervously sat down, her eyes darting around the small office while she fidgeted with the hem of her sweater. She looked pale and, noting her anxiety, I asked whether she was okay. She asked for a cup of water. When I left the room to get it for her, I asked one of the other practitioners, Kelly, who had been a nurse prior to becoming a therapist, to check on this client. At this point Corey looked worse than when she'd arrived, and Kelly asked whether she would like to lie down. As Corey nodded, I realized she was hyperventilating—a panic attack. Kelly and I immediately coached Corey to breathe slowly and helped her relax.

When she finally got some color back in her face, she apologized and said she was really nervous about therapy. I asked her whether she still needed Kelly to stay. She declined the offer. I usually do not see such an extreme reaction from clients unless they've experienced some real trauma in their lives. This time turned out to be no exception to the rule.

When she calmed down, Corey explained that her reaction was, in part, because I reminded her of someone from her past who also sported a small beard. Transference happens in therapy at times, where clients project their feelings onto their therapist and have a reaction based on the therapist's appearance or something the therapist says that reminds them of a past experience, usually a negative one.

I asked Corey if that was why she had requested a female therapist; she nodded in the affirmative. I inquired whether she might prefer to wait until a female therapist was available, but she said she needed to work this issue out, and a male therapist might be the best way to confront the demons from her childhood.

I decided not to press the issue of her past right away. I asked her general questions about her family and career. She worked as a medical technician and did not have much of a social life. She had a sister who recently moved to another state. They had always been close and still maintained contact on a daily basis, but she really missed her sister's warmth and ability to make her laugh. Her parents had divorced when Corey was a teenager and she never forgave her father for abandoning the family and running off with another woman. Five years earlier, her mother had been diagnosed with ovarian cancer and was now in remission. She helped her mother out, shuttling her to doctors' appointments and assisting with her medications.

Corey stated that she took Klonopin every morning to help manage her anxiety and at night to help her sleep. She understood the addictive nature of Klonopin, but for the time being this is what she needed in order to get by. She had been on Zoloft for years, as well, to manage her depression. Throughout college she had battled with terrible insomnia. (For those who have never experienced it, suffice it to say, it can be agonizing.)

After establishing a working rapport, I thought it would be safe to revisit Corey's strong reaction to seeing me for the first time. She said that she had been fondled by a family friend who frequently visited her home before her parents divorced. She hadn't told her mother about it until she was nineteen years old and having issues with her boyfriend: flashbacks to the incidents with the family friend. Although her mother had trouble believing Corey at first, she eventually conceded and said that if it bothered her, she would be happy to send her for therapy. Corey went for a few sessions but then stopped. Her mother promised to make sure this person would never come to the house again; besides, he had become too ill to go anywhere.

Corey breezed through college and was always at the top of her class. She was interested in nursing but decided to become a med tech instead. She had a boyfriend who she said was very understanding and a good listener. She never told her boyfriend about what had happened, but he sensed that something was wrong, as their intimate life did not seem as enjoyable as it could be.

I suggested toward the end of the session that it might be a good idea after all for Corey to see a female therapist because that may make her more comfortable in dealing with some of the intimacy issues. Corey insisted that she would like to remain with me to work primarily on her anxiety.

Corey was early for our next session. She seemed more at ease and was eager to begin. I explained to her that while it would be a good idea for us to explore the source of her anxiety, it would also be a good idea to work on practical tips for managing it. We practiced deep breathing and progressive muscle relaxation during our first few sessions. Corey proved to be a responsive client. She seemed to be managing pretty well and indicated that she was ready to explore the source of her anxiety.

Corey said that she always remembered being nervous, even before the incident with the family friend. As a young child, Corey had a difficult time separating from her mother in preschool and would often cry for long periods of time when her mother left her. She slept in the same room as her parents until she was seven years old, when her father put his foot down and said that it had to stop. She always worried about her mother. When asked about her father, she did not express the same concern.

As she grew into adolescence she became very self-conscious about her appearance and would purge her food at times. Although never formally diagnosed with an eating disorder, Corey did struggle with food issues. However, she maintained a normal body weight and exercised every day for an hour. She enjoyed running and was able to escape in that way. When her father ran away with another woman, Corey became a little rebellious and experimented with drugs. It turned out to be a very negative experience. She also met a boy whom she really liked until he tried pushing her to have sex. They eventually broke up, but the dreamy look that came over her whenever she talked about him revealed that she continued to have feelings for him. She had kept every email and text that the two had ever exchanged.

Corey described some of her fondest moments growing up. Most of them involved her grandparents on her mother's side. They were always fun, and she loved going on trips with them. Her grandfather had a quirky sense of humor and always told her funny stories.

There was also Uncle Albert, her mother's brother, whom Corey found to be pretty embarrassing. Looking back, she realized that he probably had Asperger's. He would talk about the same things over and over again and had strange, obsessive habits. One of those habits was his toenail collection. Some people hoard books and old newspapers, but Uncle Albert kept a collection of his clipped toenails—all of them! He had a set routine every day that included watching certain TV shows, and if things got off track, he would get very upset. He was also a picky eater. Heaven forbid his string beans should come into contact with anything else on his plate. Everything had to be eaten separately. Some family members would make fun of him, but even though he embarrassed her, Corey felt bad for him.

Family gatherings always included Uncle Albert, and they also included his friend. This friend seemed to know how to deal with Albert's eccentricities, but he also took an unusual interest in Corey. At first Corey thought he was nice because he would play games with her. Corey could not remember exactly when it happened, but at some point he began to touch her inappropriately and would comment on how pretty she was. She rebuffed his advances, but the experience was traumatizing for her. Eventually he stopped, and they did not speak with each other after that. Uncle Albert, all the while, never knew what was happening.

This was hard for Corey. All these years she'd had a difficult time pinpointing the source of her anxiety. She was embarrassed about Albert's strange habits, but she could not fault him for what happened with his friend. She did feel that her mother or someone in the family should have picked up on the preoccupation that Albert's friend had with her. She rationalized that perhaps if someone had paid a little more attention, nothing would have happened and she would not be in therapy today. Corey expressed intense feelings of guilt for not communicating what was happening at the house and the subsequent effects it had on her relationship with her boyfriend.

During another session, we processed what happened. I introduced a method to help inoculate her from the feelings of guilt she was experiencing. I first instructed Corey to say aloud what she felt guilty about ten times. I then asked her to repeat with increasing volume in her voice that she has accepted the past and realized that she cannot change what happened. Her mantra was "I am ready to let this go." She repeated this ten times, each time with more feeling and emotion.

Now this family friend was in a nursing home and apparently had dementia secondary to a massive stroke. Corey had contemplated visiting him but decided instead to forgive him in her mind. I used a parable to show how she had been paralyzed by the negative memories of that experience: all these years he'd been allowed to live rent-free in her mind. She realized that now she could use her mind for more fruitful endeavors.

Corey continued to process her feelings over the course of therapy. She felt guilty for a lot of things but her current guilt was how she was treating her boyfriend. She did not want to lose him and felt she needed to get help before he decided to leave her.

"He is so good to me and so patient," Corey said. "But I don't know how long he will hold out."

At the end of the session, I told Corey that it would be best if I continued to work with her on the anxiety, but I wanted to refer her to a couple's therapist to help her and her boyfriend. She agreed to the plan, and I helped get her set up for couple's therapy.

Corey continued to make progress in both therapies. Her anxiety was diminishing, and she was able to cut her doses of Klonopin in half. She felt proud of her progress but wanted to know how to deal with her boyfriend's father who reminded her of Uncle Albert in many ways, especially the way in which he ate his food. His behavior brought back a flood of memories of the abuse she had incurred at the hands of Albert's friend, and this was causing her anxiety to escalate. I told her, "Just as you are now taking your Klonopin in small doses, you need to take certain family members in small doses." I assured her that eventually the anxiety would dissipate.

During our sessions, Corey continued to speak of other aspects of her life that caused her to feel guilty. She spoke of not making the time to visit a sick relative before they had passed, the times that she experimented with marijuana, and her self-alienation from close friends. She came regularly to our sessions, and, over time, she was able to move past her troubled childhood and learned to focus on the future.

Many families experience their fair share of crises. How they respond to them will indicate their future success. In

Corey's case, her family took my suggestion and attended a support group offered at a local church and led by a very competent group therapist. When we are faced with difficult times and traumatic incidents that do not seem to go away by themselves, it is important to reach out for help. Many individuals in trauma feel very alone and isolated. Others feel embarrassed about divulging such intimate details of their lives. Those who attend a support group, or receive some form of supportive counseling, most often report back that they felt validated.

Corey and her boyfriend began getting along much better. The two of them discussed events from their pasts and mutually agreed to separate for a couple weeks while Corey worked out her most intense anxieties. Once they reconnected, their intimacy increased and many of Corey's inhibitions were lifted. She was willing to let it go. Corey had come to accept her past and move forward—in small doses.

Do You Know
the Greenbaums?

*Marriage is three parts love and seven parts
forgiveness of sins.* —Lao Tzu

I am not a great artist, but I've always enjoyed sketching. As a little boy in middle school I remember sketching pictures of rabbis with long beards and my classmates as they made silly faces. Some of my sketches captured the true essence of the person, while others were admittedly painful to look at. Certainly, Michelangelo I was not. However, my appreciation for art would prove to be a useful therapeutic technique. At times, I would sketch during therapy to demonstrate what I was seeing during the process. Regardless of the quality of my artwork, this technique can offer a fascinating revelation for the client, or client couples.

Early in my career, I developed a knack for working with couples. Some therapists don't like to work with couples or groups, but I find the dynamics of working with more than one individual at a time to be exciting.

In fact, my doctoral dissertation was a program designed to help couples through their interpersonal issues before they say "I do." I developed the program by asking 150 individuals what they felt was important to incorporate in premarital sessions, as well as what they felt was contributing to the rise in divorce, especially among Jews.

During premarital sessions, we discuss financial management, marital intimacy, communication, and dealing with in-laws, as well as the fears and anxieties that couples might have with the lifelong commitment they are about to undertake. In some cases, the couple will come to the realization on their own that the marriage was not meant to be, and they abort the relationship before making a colossal mistake. I prefer it when the couples figure it out themselves, but that does not always happen. At times, one partner is looking for the therapist to make the decision for them. There are also those rare occasions where there are so many red flags that I will insist that they terminate their relationship. But again, those are rare occasions.

Couple's therapy gives the therapist a glimpse into human behavior that you sometimes miss in individual encounters. When couples sit in front of a therapist, their true nature comes out. Real feelings of hurt are unearthed without much effort from the therapist. I view couple's therapy as a smorgasbord of all the different dishes that couples in crisis could possibly serve up to each other. These are things we see in everyday life, but they are greatly intensified during therapy.

The other enjoyable aspect of couple's therapy is the level of insight spouses have, but rarely express to each other, about their relationship. However, there are always the couples that lack any degree of insight; you just have to sit back and watch the show.

Mr. and Mrs. Bicker were referred to me by my supervisor while I was still a practicum student. I was not sure whether this supervisor was playing a practical joke on me or he just wanted to challenge me. The fact that the Bickers were Jewish might have played a role in the assignment.

When Leo and Marsha Bicker came in to my office, they were . . . bickering. (I never understood why people would pay to bicker.) They were from New York and with their heavy New York accents and silly comments, I thought this was going to be my comedic relief for the day.

They plopped themselves down on the couch, looked around for a moment and continued to talk about everything under the sun. Perhaps this is what brought them together in the first place. They both loved to talk. Listening, however, was not their forte. Talking, interrupting, talking, interrupting—it was nonstop bickering for fifteen minutes before they even acknowledged my presence.

"I didn't get your name," Leo said.

"You can call me Jonathan," I replied.

Marsha asked, "Are you a doctor?"

I informed them that I was not yet a doctor but was in school to become a psychologist. "You seem kind of young. Are you even married?"

"Yes," I replied.

"Did you go to a yeshiva (rabbinical school)?"

I replied in the affirmative to that one as well. I did not know for how long the litany of questions would go on, but I was happy to answer them. This middle-aged Jewish couple seemed intent on examining my credentials to see whether I was worthy of counseling them. I had to grant them that courtesy.

Leo said to Marsha, "Give the guy a chance. You don't let anyone *tawlk*."

This comment led to another fifteen minutes of bickering between Leo and Marsha about who gets to talk and when. With my pad in front of me, I was very tempted to write what I had once seen in a Far Side cartoon: "Just plain nuts!" Instead, I sketched. I continued sketching Leo and Marsha while they bickered about everything from my credentials to Bill Clinton. (To this day I don't know how Bill Clinton made it into the conversation!) I am very good at remaining poker-faced when people say things that make no logical sense. But the longer they continued their verbal onslaught, the harder it was to keep a neutral expression.

I continued to struggle to find any connection or flow in Leo and Marsha's conversation, if you could call it that. Finally, after another quarter hour, I finished my sketch and said to them, "Our time is almost up so I want to summarize what we have accomplished today."

Leo looked up at me and said, "Accomplished? You have not said a word. I can't believe we are actually paying for this bogus session."

Marsha responded in her thick accent, "Well, you didn't let him *tawlk*." (Jerry Seinfeld would have loved this couple.) Marsha said, "Okay, we'll shut up now. But I'm just curious. Where ya from?"

"Baltimore," I said.

"Oh! Do you know the Greenbaums from *Bawl*timore? They probably go to the same shul (synagogue) as you."

"Shut up Marsha and let the man talk!" Leo screamed.

Finally, I conducted my insight-filled summary into Leo and Marsha's marital issues. I turned over my pad. "While you were having your conversation, I was taking some notes," I said, doing my best to contain myself.

"Notes! Those don't look like notes. You were drawing all this time! Is that what we paid you to do?"

"I want you to look at this sketch a little more carefully and tell me what you see," I said, trying to keep this ADD poster couple a little more focused.

They moved closer to my chair and Marsha said, "It kinda looks like us although my nose is definitely not that big. And is my hair really that light? I just dyed it *yestaday!*"

I was tempted to make a crack but I continued. "I want you to look more carefully at the sketch and notice your body positions."

"Yeah, what about it?" Leo asked.

"Notice that although you are sitting on the same couch, you are not facing each other. In fact, you never made eye contact with each other this whole hour."

"Yeah, and therefore? I've seen enough of this man (pointing to Leo)." Marsha pressed on, "Why do you people think that we always need to look at each other? My parents didn't look at each other. That's what people do in the movies. Do you watch movies by the way?"

I ignored her and continued. "Well, you see, this is what you looked like to me during the past fifty minutes. If this is what you looked like to me, this is probably how others perceive you as a couple."

Leo piped up and said, "Is that what you think our problem is? We don't look at each other?"

"That is part of the problem," I responded. "But it seems like you two don't know how to fight."

"Don't know how to fight? Are you kidding? That's all we know how to do. We could teach you if you want," quipped Marsha, laughing out loud.

"But you do not know how to have a fair fight. You see, animals typically do not use eye contact as a method of communicating their wants and needs. We, as humans, were created quite differently. When we communicate, we have the ability to show ourselves through our eyes.

When you argue while looking at each other, you establish a more meaningful connection and are therefore working on the same playing field." (I was proud of my interpretation and insightful comments.)

Leo nodded his head as if to give the impression that he was internalizing what I had just said. In reality, he was looking at my watch.

"That's a Kenneth Cole, right?" remarked Leo. (I honestly had no clue of the brand. My wife had bought it for me.)

I steered them back to the topic of therapy and asked them what they wanted to get out of the session.

Marsha chimed in, "You are supposed to fix him," pointing at Leo. I attempted to explain to her about how couple's therapy works and how it takes two to tango.

I thought I was making some headway when Marsha turned to me and said, "You still didn't answer my question. Do you know the Greenbaums from *Bawl*timore or not?"

Leo and Marsha returned for two more sessions before I let my supervisor know that therapy was getting nowhere. Their level of insight and psychological sophistication was about a negative 2 on a scale from 1 to 10.

Reflecting back on the Bickers, I came to several realizations. I realized that I prefer working with motivated people. I realized that couples have no shame when they are in the heat of an argument. And finally, I realized that by challenging me with this difficult couple, my supervisor had given me the opportunity to see there's sometimes another take on couple's therapy.

I'm at Your Front Door

Most people think they are searching for truth when they are really searching for love.—Harold Clemp

Every therapist has their fair share of clients who become dependent on them. Barb was one such client. Barb had been through therapists like most people go through toilet paper. She typically chose male therapists, but I only learned that later as we navigated the sometimes murky waters of therapy. Barb was a schoolteacher who presented with an "eating disorder," as she put it on the referral form. She also stated that she suffered from depression and was hospitalized on more than one occasion for what she called "nervous breakdowns." (Of course, the term *nervous breakdown* has a different meaning to each individual.)

At first, Barb seemed like a motivated client. She came early to appointments and would pretend to be reading the outdated magazines in the very outdated waiting room.

Whenever someone would come into the room to wait for their therapist, Barb would strike up a conversation with them whether they were interested or not. She'd make inappropriate comments and ask personal questions of those around her. She'd make many trips to the water cooler as well, which would also lead to many bathroom visits. Sometimes clients would complain about Barb because she was so nosy and intrusive and just made them more anxious than they already were. On the other hand, Barb seemed to really enjoy the whole therapy experience.

I personally do not like to have too much information about a client before seeing them because I like to formulate my own opinions about them without being clouded by the judgment of others. Barb came into the office for her first session and looked around for a couple of minutes. "I would never have chosen these colors for a therapy room," she said. "Neither would I," I responded with a smile. (At the time, I was sharing space with another therapist, and I was not in charge of the decor. However, how an office is decorated is something I try to take seriously. It can affect the treatment in many ways. If the walls have too much on them, they can serve as a distraction. If the lights are too bright, they can cause pain sufferers even more discomfort. Your ability to control for these factors largely depends on whether you share space with others.)

Barb was somewhat overweight but dressed well and wore lots of makeup and perfume. (I am very sensitive to perfumes, and she did not choose one that I could handle in the large doses that she applied.) She began by asking me where I went to school and whether I had experience treating people with eating disorders. I told her the name of the school I attended, which did not seem to make much of an impression on her. I also told her that I indeed had experience working with people suffering from eating disorders, although it was not my specialty. She went on to describe her problem with food, that she could not control her weight and that she needed help. I stated that I would do my best. (In the United States the eating disorder that affects more individuals than any other is obesity. However, it is not commonly referred to as an eating disorder. In my book, anything that impairs a person from functioning close to their capacity is a disorder and worthy of treatment. Barb was by no means morbidly obese, but she was clearly overweight.)

The session continued with my taking a detailed history from Barb and her peppering me with personal questions about my religious affiliation and my family. Each time I attempted to steer her back to discussing her issues, she would somehow manage to slip in another question about me. I decided to process the immediacy issues and asked her what she was feeling right then that was causing her to ask such personal questions. She stated that she had been burnt by therapists before, so she wanted to make sure that I would be a good match for her. This sounded like a reasonable response.

As our sessions progressed, I learned more about Barb, her family, and her obsessions with food. She took me through her personal history of being bullied in school and having trouble finding jobs. She felt that she was not being hired because employers looked at her weight and turned her down because of it. She also mentioned that she had suicidal thoughts on many occasions.

We explored her suicidality, and she assured me that she was not planning to commit suicide.

The compliments began toward the end of our fourth session. She ended the session by stating that she had never felt so comfortable with a therapist before and that she felt I would be the one to finally help her. I thanked her for her kind words. I told her that it might not necessarily be my efforts that were contributing to this feeling and that there were many other competent therapists out there. I also mistakenly told her that her efforts and motivation to get help were paying off for her. She smiled and walked out the door.

The following week was my birthday. I did not share this with Barb, but I did tell her that I would not be available for her weekly session and offered her another day to meet with me. On my birthday I received a card in the mail. Usually I do not get birthday cards from anyone in the mail, with the exception of my parents—who have never missed a year. I opened the card and immediately scanned down to the bottom and read *Fondly, Barb*. I am not sure how she found out when my birthday was, although in this day and age you can find out almost anything about anyone. The card contained a humorous greeting and a personal, handwritten note of thanks.

I contemplated how I would deal with the birthday card during the next session. I decided not to bring it up unless she did. She did. "Did you like the card?" she asked. I said it was a very nice card but it was unnecessary. I also informed her that she should not send me cards in the future because I would like to keep our relationship professional and that sending a birthday card to my house was a bit much. She seemed upset, but I felt that I had to set boundaries as early as possible.

About a month later I was invited to give a lecture for a local organization. I got up to the podium, and, to my shock, there was Barb in the audience. I did not know that Barb had any interest in psychology . . . but there she was. The only interests that she had expressed to me in therapy were becoming a manicurist and opening a restaurant. After my lecture, she came over to me and said she had never heard such a good lecture. I was concerned that she would speak to me in a way that would indicate that she was my client. I try to keep the public from recognizing who my clients are to protect their confidentiality, so I quickly thanked her for her kind words and walked out. I suspect that Barb had some sort of secret satisfaction from letting people know that I was her therapist, but I decided not to explore it, instead keeping it on the back burner to be revisited at a later date.

During our next session, Barb commented how she had lost fifteen pounds since we began therapy. She wanted to know whether I had noticed. I was afraid she would ask that question. I just smiled and said, "That must make you feel really good. Keep up the good work." The flat expression on her face made me feel that I had not given her the attention she was looking for. I made a note to discuss Barb's behavior toward me with my supervisor. My ongoing concerns about Barb's poor boundaries and insistence on seeing me more than was therapeutically necessary or even helpful concerned me. I therefore suggested to Barb that we meet every other week, which she flat out rejected. She said that she really enjoyed our sessions and did not want to "lose the momentum."

The following week, I met with my supervisor and described Barb and her continual barrage of personal questions. I also mentioned the birthday card and the lecture that Barb somehow managed to find out about. My supervisor confirmed my suspicions that Barb most likely had a borderline personality disorder (BPD). She advised me to proceed with caution. I asked whether I could refer her to someone else to which my supervisor said unequivocally, *no*. "This will be a good learning experience for you, Jonathan." I halfheartedly thanked her and left.

The weekly sessions continued, and Barb continued to lose weight. Her interest in my personal life subsided somewhat, until one day when she met one of my children. During the summer that I first began seeing Barb, our family took a trip to Hershey Park. It was a nice getaway, although I am not a big fan of amusement parks. One of my children begged me to go on a particular ride with her, and I finally gave in. Sitting next to me on the ride was none other than . . . you guessed it—Barb! With me a huge smile she said, "Hi there, Dr. Lasson. Is this your daughter? She is so cute." She continued to ask my daughter questions about where she went to school and what her favorite ride was at the park. Meanwhile I was thinking about the quickest way to get a restraining order. She then told my daughter, "Your dad is a great psychologist!" My daughter was young at the time and, not really knowing what Barb was talking about, went on to the next ride. I shot Barb a look to let her know that this would be discussed later (unless the restraining order would be in place prior to the next scheduled session!).

The dreaded next session came the following week. Barb came in and immediately disarmed me. "I am so sorry about what happened at Hershey Park. I honestly did not know you were going to be there. I will never do that again." There went my processing of the situation. I had prepared a whole lecture where I would clearly restate the boundaries. I did not get my chance. Instead, Barb went on to tell me that she did not feel depressed anymore. She was effusive with her praise of my skills. (I am still not sure which skills she was referring to.)

Our uneventful therapy sessions continued for about a month. I noticed that Barb would extend the sessions till the last possible minute and would sometimes ask if she could have a double session so she would have more time to talk about her issues. When I told her that I did not think that would be a good idea, she confided in me that she had become more suicidal lately. She said that she'd just broken up with her boyfriend and needed to talk things over. The next session she showed me a superficial cut near her wrist and said she had begun cutting herself because it took away the emotional pain from the breakup. I made her fill out an anti-suicide contract, as directed by my supervisor.

She said she was not planning on committing suicide, but I was not taking any chances. My experience with suicidal clients has led me to be extra judicious as a way of protecting the client, as well as shielding myself from the guilt I would have to deal with if the client were successful with their suicide.

The following week, I received the emergency call at three in the morning. On the other end of the line I could barely make out a voice, so I hung up. The phone rang again, and this time the voice was clear. It was Barb. She said she could not stand it anymore and wanted to kill herself. I asked her where she was at that moment. She replied, "I'm at your front door."

"Of my office?" I asked, half asleep.

"No. Your house."

I quickly got dressed, trying not to wake up my family, and ran to the front door. Sure enough, there was Barb. She was smiling and thanked me profusely for answering. "I was really feeling lousy, but I wasn't really going to kill myself. I just needed to talk to you."

At three in the morning most people do not think rationally. I tried my best to keep my composure and told her in a calm but stern voice, "Barb, you are never to come over to my house again. Do you understand me? I will talk with you about this later."

As soon as I woke up from a lousy night of sleep, I put in a call to my supervisor to discuss what happened. She felt terrible that I was being put through this and gave me suggestions as to how to terminate therapy with Barb. I was nervous about the repercussions of terminating, but I knew that things were getting out of hand.

When Barb came back for what I thought would be our final session, she immediately apologized to me and pleaded with me not to terminate her. She said she was really feeling down and she just wanted to talk to me and that she would never do that again. I said that I'd have to think about it. This was the second time she promised not to engage in boundary-crossing behavior. I told her that I would let her know my decision before our next session. Barb began to cry. I sat in silence, watching her cry and occasionally blow her nose. After what seemed like forever, Barb handed me a handwritten apology note that she had written before the session. In the note, she mentioned once again that she felt I was the only one who could possibly help her. She got up and left.

In general, I have a soft heart for people in desperate situations. Individuals with borderline personality disorder are very complicated in their presentation and the treatment options for BPD do not always give a therapist hope for a successful outcome. I consulted with a colleague who had many years of experience with individuals with BPD. He suggested that if I were to agree to continue treating Barb, I would need her to sign an agreement outlining what is considered appropriate and what is not. He also recommended that I read up on Dialectical Behavioral Therapy, which is one of the most common treatment modalities used in working with individuals with BPD. It focuses on mindfulness, learning how to control deep emotions, reducing self-destructive behavior and managing stress. I was not sure whether or not this approach would work with Barb, but I was willing to give it a try.

Barb never ended up calling for another appointment. The next time I saw her was at a restaurant almost two years after our last face-to-face session. She had her arm around a young man and proudly introduced him as her fiancé. She introduced me as her former therapist who saved her life. I was happy that she had found love . . . in someone aside from me.

I had always been told by my teachers and supervisors that individuals with borderline personalities can be a psychologist's worst nightmare. You sometimes have to become a different person when working with such clients. You must be very stern and up front about what the rules and expectations are in therapy. There is also a higher likelihood that these individuals will make false allegations about their therapists if they do not get what they want, which is usually more than just a therapeutic relationship. Barb made many attempts to get into my personal life, which caused me to question my abilities at times. I had to recognize that this was my issue and not Barb's. She was just acting in the way she had been conditioned to act for many years. It was a great learning lesson for me, and I was happy that I stayed the course—and that Barb moved to New Zealand.

CAR WASHES

Instead of thinking outside of the box, get rid of the box.
—Deepak Chopra

When working with inner city students, you sometimes have no choice as to where you will be placed. Before the advent of GPS systems and satellite images, we had to physically go to a location to know what it was like. Because I always wanted to know where my placement was situated before the school year began, I would scout out the area and familiarize myself with the school and its surroundings.

One of my first assignments was at a school in a neighborhood fraught with drugs, prostitution and high crime. The school was across from a liquor store, a check-cashing operation, and a bail bondsman. These are not the typical establishments you would find in upscale neighborhoods, but they dot the streets of Baltimore, especially the North Avenue corridor.

Driving my Honda to the school, I tried to find a spot as near to the entrance as possible, but the closest I could find was a good two blocks away. Reluctantly, I parked my car and got out.

Coming up the street toward me were three rough-looking young men who stared me up and down. One of them glanced behind him to scan whether anyone else was around. I was nervous. It was my first day working at this school, and I was sure I was about to get mugged.

I thought back to my days of taking martial arts classes and teaching martial arts at a summer camp. I had never used this knowledge in a real-life situation. I was not about to use it on that day either. Besides, if it were only one or two, perhaps I could handle myself. But a three-on-one—forget it! And who knew what types of weapons they might be carrying? I whispered a quiet prayer and hoped for the best.

My first sensei had taught me how to de-escalate potentially violent situations with words. I don't know where I came up with the idea, but it was clear that some higher power had my back.

As the group neared, they surrounded me on all three sides. I smiled at them and, before they could say anything, I said, "Hey guys. I am new to this school and am kind of nervous about leaving my car here. Do you mind keeping an eye on it from time to time?"

They looked at each other. The leader who was facing me said, "I'll make you a deal. Give me thirty bucks a month and I'll make sure nothing happens to your car. I'll even throw in a monthly car wash."

I quickly took out thirty dollars and handed it to the gentleman. "Deal!" He asked, "You really workin' here?"

"Yup," I said. The leader then asked, "What do I call you?"

"You can call me Doc," I replied.

I walked away thankful for getting out of that situation. It had turned out great—I had my own private security detail, and a car detail thrown in!

I walked into the school building and introduced myself quickly to the principal. I could tell she was busy with new parents trying to find out where their children would be that year. So I found another woman who looked equally lost and asked her whether she had any idea where service providers, such as speech pathologists and school psychologists, had their offices. She walked me to the back of the building and pointing to the corner said, "That desk is open. You can use it." The desk looked like it had seen better years. Two of its drawers were missing, and the computer sitting on top of it had no wires connected. I realized that I would have to put together my own office.

I found the maintenance man, and he kindly showed me to a storage closet. "Take whatever you need before everyone else gets to it," he advised. Thanking him I walked into the storage closet.

The stench was overwhelming. A school social worker was in the closet as well. She laughed when she saw me holding my nose. "What? You don't like the smell of weed?" She burst out laughing and introduced herself. We became instant friends. I found the wires and cables I needed and hurried out of the closet.

There were no other options in terms of office space. I wondered where I could see students that afforded some level of privacy. As was becoming evident, having your own office space was a luxury. Walking around the school I noticed a room right off the gymnasium that seemed suitable for my purposes. I asked the principal whether I could use it. She said it was okay unless they had an event going on in the gymnasium, which was really a multipurpose room.

When I get to a new school, I like to get to work right away. I combed through the files of the students who would be on my caseload for that year and chose a third-grader as my first student to counsel. His Individualized Education Plan (IEP) stated that he took medication for Attention Deficit Hyperactivity Disorder (ADHD). His name was Darius and by age nine, I think he had exhausted every stimulant out there, with very little success. There seemed to be many students on my caseload with a diagnosis of ADHD, students whom the social worker referred to as the "methylphenidate crew."

Darius' classroom was in chaos. A new teacher was in front of the room, clearly competing for the award of "teacher who lasted less than five minutes at school." I called out the name Darius; two boys came over to me. "Which Darius you lookin' for?"

I said the last name and a wide-eyed boy raised his hand. He looked much younger than nine years old, so I asked him to repeat his last name to be sure. I said, "I'm going to borrow you for a little bit. Is that okay?" The teacher just waved at me and tried again to restore order.

In the hallway, Darius sweetly asked, "Who are you?"

"My name is Dr. Lasson. I am the new psychologist this year."

"You mean I ain't going with Ms. Jen this year?" Darius asked with a hint of sadness. I said, "No, Ms. Jen is working at another school, but she told me to say *hi*."

"Okay," he murmured. "She was nice and we played fun games. Do you got Uno?"

"No, but I will make sure to bring it next time. I do have some other games, but I want to get to know you today. This is my first time at this school."

He looked around and said, "It's all right."

"Where are we goin'?" Ms. Jen's office is the other way," asked Darius while looking around.

"We are going to meet in a room near the gym. It's much quieter there and maybe we can shoot some hoops later."

"I got a really good shot, but I am kinda short."

"That's okay." I told him that I had always been the shortest kid in my class until the ninth grade. He nodded.

I made a mental note to call Ms. Jen to ask her more about Darius.

We talked a little bit, and then he quietly shot some hoops. He stood in almost the same exact spot every time he would shoot the basketball. I found this kind of interesting and took a mental note to address this later.

Darius proved to be a bright young man who had a difficult time sitting still. I was curious to know how bright he was and leafed through his IEP folder. By third grade he already had a Volume 2 to his folder, which was filled with many IEPs and other documents. I flipped to the assessment section and learned that Darius had an IQ of 118, which meant that he was in the high average range. Darius was receiving special educational services in the area of mathematics. Children with ADHD generally do poorly in mathematics as math requires the ability to sustain attention and maintain focus.

The next session I brought the Uno game, recently purchased at the nearby Dollar Store because the set at school was missing about 100 of the 108 cards. Darius was excited that I remembered to bring the game. I asked Darius if he could first draw me some pictures. Darius said that he was not a great artist. I encouraged him to do his best. He started with a house. I noticed him looking around the room, so I asked, "Do you need something?"

"Yeah, a ruler," was his reply. I didn't see one around and thought that was a rather odd request. I promised him that next time I would have a ruler. Darius continued drawing and erasing, drawing and erasing. It took almost twenty minutes for him to complete only part of the house to his satisfaction. I told him that he could continue his picture next time. He begged me to stay a few more minutes. I figured that his teacher, who still could not manage the classroom, would probably not mind, let alone notice if Darius was missing for a little longer. We continued working until his lunch break.

Over lunch I took out his file and read through some of the past reports. Darius had six siblings, some half and some full. He had been in and out of foster homes over the past couple years. His mother suffered from schizophrenia and his father was deceased. He was being cared for by a foster parent, whom I recalled having seen pick him up a couple days earlier.

Darius had been born prematurely and suffered from malnutrition, which explained his short stature. His file mentioned that he also experienced tics, which could have been related to the medication he was on. I had never noticed any tics while working with him. I put in a call to Ms. Jen.

When Jen and I spoke, I informed her that I was still working with Darius and that he seemed to be connecting well with me.

"Did you play him Uno? He loves Uno."

"Not yet, but probably soon," I answered.

I asked Jen whether she knew anything about Darius' father. She knew little other than the fact that he was murdered shortly after Darius was born. "Darius craves male attention," Jen surmised, "as a result of growing up without a father." I then asked why she thought the medications were doing so little to help him. She said that he did not always take them, and his foster mom had become concerned when he developed the tics. I mentioned that I had not noticed any tics. She went on to say that Darius sometimes appears to be talking to himself. I had not noticed this either but remembered that his mother had a significant mental health history.

The next time I picked up Darius from his classroom I noticed there was already a new teacher. The first one lasted about one month. I wondered how long this next one would last.

As I walked Darius down to the gym, I took more notice of his mannerisms. He walked with his head looking down to the floor and his lips were moving. I asked him if he was saying something. He said "No, just counting." We stopped walking.

"What are you counting?"

"Tiles. I always do."

"That's interesting," I said. "Let's keep going."

He did this the entire way to the gym. When we got there I asked him how many tiles there were. He said, "248." I asked him why he counted tiles. "It calms me down," he said. We talked a bit more about the things that cause him stress. He said that he did not like loud noises or when there was lots of mess and trash all over. I asked him if he kept his room neat. He did.

We played a game of Uno, and then he went back to class.

Sitting at my desk in the room with the other related service providers, I asked if anyone else had worked with Darius. No one seemed to know much about this child other than the fact that he had an older brother who lived nearby and that they saw each other occasionally. I asked what the brother did, and the social worker said that he washed cars and other odd jobs but had his run-ins with law enforcement. I wondered to myself whether he was the one who washed my car every month.

It turned out that Darius' brother and almost all of his relatives had trouble with the law. Under the mayor's "zero tolerance" crusade, many young black men were being arrested for minor offenses. The mayor's program did not seem to be working out too well for this West Baltimore community.

I certainly was hoping that Darius would turn out okay, so I put more energy into his particular case. If all the medications were not helping him, and he had negative side effects with some of them, perhaps ADHD was not the proper diagnosis. I have never been a big fan of diagnostic labels, and this label had followed Darius throughout this IEP. In fact, he had been taking stimulant medications since he was four years old!

I asked his foster mother to sign a release for me to speak to his treating physician, which she gladly did. I called the doctor who was a fellow at the University of Maryland Hospital and was told to call back at lunchtime the following day.

When I reached the doctor, I was impressed with his knowledge of Darius. He said that he really liked him and was open to suggestions. I explained what I had noticed and suggested that perhaps Darius did not have a classic ADHD presentation. "If he does not have ADHD, what do you think it might be?" he asked.

"I think that Darius has more of an anxiety disorder than attention-related issues." I went through the history of medications that failed him, and we discussed an alternative treatment plan that would introduce antidepressants with an anti-anxiety component instead of the stimulants. He thought about it and said he would get back to me after he saw Darius the next week.

A few days later the doctor called and said that he had talked it over with another psychiatrist, and they agreed to give Darius a trial of Luvox. This was the medication I was hoping they would suggest because I had seen positive results with some of my private clients who took it. I explained to the doctor that I felt his symptoms were more indicative of anxiety and obsessive-compulsive traits.

The results were not immediate, but Darius' foster parent kept with the regimen. Slowly the anxiety symptoms dissipated, and Darius began to function better both at home and in school. One day when we were going down to the gym, I noticed Darius was no longer counting tiles. I asked him why he wasn't counting anymore. "It's a waste of time," he said. I continued working with Darius the following year and told him that I was coming to his fifth-grade graduation.

Darius indeed graduated at the top of his class. He found me in the crowd and smiled.

Clinicians have to think out of the box if they are to be successful in real-life situations, especially in dealing with unconventional children. Thinking out of the box earned me better results from my students and I believe, it earned me my own personal security detail.

I'm Glad
I Cured You

Don't feel sorry for yourself if you have chosen the wrong road.
Turn around! —Edgar Cayee

Teenagers don't just wake up and ask their parents if they can go for therapy, although there may be some rare exceptions. I often get a very surprised look when I tell my students that one of my favorite populations to work with is the "angry teen" population. You might be thinking, aren't all teens angry? The answer is flat out *NO*!

My students will incredulously ask, why would anyone want to work with angry people, let alone angry teens? Most rational people, if given the option of working with an enraged teen or voluntarily having their brain removed, would choose the latter. For some reason I have always felt that there was something tangible about rage, especially in teens. Angry people in general have reasons to be irate. They are not always rational to us, but at least in their minds their anger makes perfect sense. The world has done them an injustice. Their parents have done them an injustice. Their teachers have committed an injustice. You see, teenagers, for the most part are still subject to more rules than those over eighteen. They are constantly being told what they cannot do. Regardless, angry people, from my point of view, are easier to deal with then, say, people who are depressed. People with depression generally lack the motivation to truly express what they are feeling and thinking. Angry people are far more capable of emotional expression.

Joe was an angry teenager—a seventeen-year-old who did not wake up one morning and tell his parents that he wanted to see a shrink. Most teens I see are forced to come to me. They are failing school and need testing. Or they were arrested for driving under the influence and need to come for therapy so they can have their ankle bracelet removed. Or they are court-ordered to come for therapy. The one thing they all have in common: they don't come because they want to be there.

I had very little information about Joe prior to our first encounter, which is how I prefer it. His mother was very curt on the phone and when his father tried to interject a positive quality about Joe, he was quickly shut down by an obviously livid mother. How they got to me was an interesting story in itself.

I'd attended a conference in Maryland on dealing with teens. Among the participants was a social worker who primarily dealt with intellectually limited adults and who was having difficulty dealing with her own family. Her long work hours didn't allow her to be part of Joe's life and the time they did spend together was contentious.

At the end of the conference, we were mingling and having coffee when Joe's mother approached me. She had heard my contribution to the discussion of working with teens during a presentation at the conference. Apparently, I had mentioned that I work primarily with unconventional teens and practiced in the Baltimore area. She said that she wanted to speak with me and possibly make an appointment for her son. And, so I met Joe.

Joe was committed to giving this shrink a hard time. *Shrink* was the name that many teens fondly give to therapists. Joe had been kicked out of school for the fourth time in one year and was not being allowed back until he got the all-clear from the shrink. (What a great job I have—giving all-clears when I have no clue whatsoever whether the kid will commit some act of stupidity again.)

Apparently, the ride over to my office was not one you would see in a Brady Bunch family trip. Angry Joe was driven to my office by his equally angry mother. I learned later from the receptionist that Joe's mother whispered loud enough for those in the next building over, "You better talk to this one or else." We were off to a great start, and Joe had not even taken a seat. Joe came into my office without making any eye contact or even saying *hello*. As a therapist familiar working with adolescents, I was used to these warm fuzzy beginnings; Joe's demeanor did not phase me.

I opened with my typical confidentiality *spiel*, which Joe had probably heard a dozen times before from other unsuccessful therapists. I then asked my next typical question: "What brings you here today, Joe?" No response. "Okay," I continued, "If your mom were in this room right now, what would she say you are coming to see me about?"

Still no response. Joe was determined. I strategically turned the other way and sat at my writing desk and scribbled some notes about Joe being a non-compliant teenager. I then read some emails and an article that I had been in the middle of before Joe's mother rudely interrupted me by bringing in her angry teen. After about twenty-five minutes, I turned to see Joe who was still slumped on the couch playing with his cell phone and said, "Well our time is just about up. It was nice meeting you. I am glad I was able to cure you."

He looked up at me and said, "What are you talking about. I didn't say a word to you. You didn't do crap!"

"Well, actually I did." (Pause) I continued, "You see, when you came here today, you were determined that you were not going to talk to some stupid shrink. You held your own and succeeded in not talking to me. So, you won. It must make you feel happy to win. So in a sense I also won."

Joe looked confused. "What are you talking about?"

"Well, part of my job is making angry people like you . . . happy. You won—you're happy. You're happy—I did my job. I won too."

Full eye contact now from Joe. "That is one of the craziest, things I've ever heard," and he burst out laughing.

Making progress, I continued with my plan. "I'll make you a deal. You don't have to ever come back and see me again, but I don't want you to make a decision yet. I want you to go home and think about it, and call me if you want to schedule another appointment so we can help each other some more." Smiling, he took my business card and left. He came back the following week and became one of my most motivated clients. All I had to do to accomplish this was to give Joe a small taste of victory . . . and a good dose of humor.

Over the course of our sessions together I came to learn that Joe was most angry about the unrealistic rules that his parents placed on him. He wanted to be free to express himself, and they were clamping down on him. He was giving it right back to them. We discussed his distaste for authority. We talked about his future and how he would handle being a parent. Being a parent was not in his immediate plans, so we discussed the idea of simply graduating from high school. Although Joe was a very bright and capable young man, he was having trouble getting along with some teachers. So I arranged a meeting with the principal, who was more than willing to accommodate my request. From then on he allowed Joe to work with a tutor instead of attending the actual classes, where he had most of his conflicts.

We also discussed how Joe never was able to match up to his older brother who was, in his words, a "goody two shoes" who always did the right thing and never got in trouble. He and his brother had very little in common with the exception of their mutual love for music. Joe learned to appreciate his brother over time and even allowed his brother to teach him the guitar.

Joe and I continued to work together on his issues with authority. We processed his feelings of anger toward his mother, which were primarily rooted in the idea that she was never available for him and never appreciated his friends or his music. After a few months, I arranged to have his mother come in for half of the session. I prepared her for the fact that Joe would likely express his anger toward her and that her role would be to simply acknowledge and apologize. I cautioned her against using any psychological terms, as she would frequently do because of her work as a social worker. She followed my advice to a tee, and later, in a phone conversation, I congratulated her for behaving herself.

The school year was coming to an end and Joe had made significant progress. He understood that he won't always like what is said to him, but he should see it as a means to an end and comply. I watched him accept his diploma from high school. He looked at me from the stage and he mouthed a "Thank you" in my direction. It was a happy moment—a win for both of us.

Reflecting back on my work with Joe, I pondered the nature of resistance and its role in therapy. There is no official guidebook or script with directions on what to say to a resistant client, especially a resistant teen. You can't google it. There are no YouTube demonstrations that adequately depict how to counter the resistance. Sometimes, you just have to get creative. The savory taste of victory—that was all Joe needed. I have learned that when I put in the effort and keep an open-minded approach, the right words—and rewards—will eventually come.

Caught in
a Guilt Trap

*If we climb high enough, we will reach a height from which
tragedy ceases to look tragic.* —Irvin D. Yalom

Teaching college classes has been a very rewarding experience for me. I enjoy the give and take during class discussions, and teaching forces me to be creative, innovative, and engaging. There is nothing worse for a teacher than disengaged students who are busy trying to find Pokemon on their iPhones while tuning out someone rambling about Freud in the background.

I truly care about my students and their success. Taking the time to get to know each of them pays off in many ways. Sometimes, once they are no longer in your class, they end up becoming your clients. Such was the case with Alexis.

Alexis was one of the top students in my Social Psychology class. Always engaged, she loved hearing about interesting social psychology experiments. She was particularly intrigued by the bystander effect and raised very poignant questions. I remember one day she asked, "Dr. Lasson, I think I understand why people don't take action, but I wonder what the characteristics are of those who do in fact take action in emergency situations." I had always questioned this, as well, and was glad to have the chance to discuss the topic.

Two years after taking my class, Alexis called me. She said that she'd really enjoyed my class and wanted to know if she could schedule an appointment with me. We scheduled to meet on a Sunday morning because Alexis was working most of the week as a special education teacher.

Alexis presented herself well. Although I am usually not very good with recognizing faces, I could tell that she had not changed much. Her curious eyes and fair complexion were the same as I remembered.

She sat down and briefly looked around the office. "Your office is different from what I had expected," she commented.

"What did you expect it to look like?" I asked.

"I never thought you were the type that would have a pink carpet and dancing shoes." I explained to her that I shared space with another clinician. She smiled and looked down.

"So Alexis, what brings you here today?" Alexis looked up and immediately began to cry. I have that effect on people sometimes. Handing her the box of tissues, I waited for her sobbing to abate.

"I am so embarrassed. I went to a couple of other therapists, but I did not connect with them and I remembered our class and our discussions and I thought I would give it one last shot."

"Does that mean you were ready to give up?" I could see the pain in her eyes. She continued, "There are some mornings that I wish I would not wake up." I was curious to know what she could be going through that was so painful. She seemed to have it all, but I have learned that humans are far more complex than they appear on the outside, and we, as therapists, should not make any generalizations. I encouraged her to continue.

"I came to you because I felt you could understand me better than the other therapists," she said.

"Why would you think I could understand you any better than other therapists?" I asked curiously.

"Because of our discussion on the bystander effect that we had in Social Psychology. I have been dealing with feelings of guilt for such a long time. When we discussed those who do take action it got me thinking. I started to do things that I had never done before. I began to help people even if it did not seem like a major emergency. I would walk downtown handing out sandwiches to homeless people. I began picking up trash from the floor when it was not my job to do so. I became compulsive about cleanliness. I wanted to do my best to make the world a little better place."

At this point I was amazed at how Alexis had changed just based on a discussion in class. Teaching is so powerful, I realized, and I never want to give it up. However, inasmuch as Alexis was doing so many wonderful things for society, she was still in lots of pain.

Alexis told me more about her background. She came from a middle-to upper-class family in Virginia. Her parents worked hard and were successful to a point, but they abhorred wealth. They taught their children values and strong work ethic by example. Her father started out as a stock boy in a store and rose in the ranks to manager. He eventually owned three hardware stores and truly enjoyed what he did. Her mother was a librarian at a local college and an avid reader and gardener. She was a mild-mannered woman; Alexis could not recall her mother ever saying a bad word about anyone. She was truly a role model for Alexis. Alexis would accompany her mother to church, and although she did not enjoy the services, she saw the reverence her parents, especially her mother, had for God and the pastor.

Alexis had two siblings, Anna and Brian. Alexis spoke about how much she loved her siblings and how she thought she had the perfect family. They went on amazing family trips where they had fun singing together in the car and making funny faces at each other. They played board games and loved being out in nature. The three of them, with their different personalities, all complemented each other in wonderful ways. They were very happy—until tragedy struck.

One summer day while vacationing in Orlando, Alexis and her family, after a long, hot day at the Disney parks came back to their vacation home. Her mother asked Alexis to watch her siblings while she and her father prepared supper. Alexis was fourteen and Anna and Brian were eleven and seven, respectively. Alexis went outside to the pool, and Anna and Brian joined her for a swim to cool off. At some point Alexis got out and lay down on a lounge chair. Not realizing how tired she was, she closed her eyes and soon fell asleep.

Anna had also gotten out of the pool to use the bathroom, leaving Brian by himself. When Anna came back outside, she found Brian face down in the water. She screamed for Alexis. Alexis jumped up and saw, to her horror, that Brian was not moving. She screamed for help as she jumped into the pool. Her parents came out and tried to resuscitate Brian. They called 911 and the medics took over, but it was too late. Brian was declared brain dead. He remained comatose for two weeks before he passed away.

Alexis sobbed as she retold this painful tragedy, and I could not help but dry my own eyes. I could not imagine the intense feelings of guilt that probably consumed Alexis ever since Brian's death. It was no wonder she had so many days when she did not want to wake up.

Since Brian's death, the family changed. Although her parents never blamed Alexis for her brother's death, she always felt that it was her fault. Her mother explained that God has plans for everyone and that it was Brian's time to go. Alexis was amazed that her mother could remain so faithful despite losing her only son. At Brian's funeral, her mother and father both spoke after the pastor finished speaking. Alexis was almost inconsolable, but she was determined to read a poem that she had written about the loss of her dear brother. Her father was never the same after the accident. Once a doting father, he became withdrawn and depressed. The loss of Brian killed him mentally and eventually physically. At age forty-eight, Alexis' father died of a heart attack.

There are points in a therapist's career where the stories told are so heartbreaking that the therapist needs time to process and consult. Alexis' story was one of those that I had to share with colleagues. Seeing Alexis feeling so guilty was very painful to watch. No amount of training prepares a therapist for heart-wrenching stories. We just have to take stock and process our own feelings and, . . . yes, . . . even cry from time to time.

At the end of the session, Alexis looked spent. She said that she had never told this story to anyone. I was surprised and Alexis saw my look. She said, "I have pretended that I never had a little brother for many years, and now I need to face the demons of the past." Guilt-ridden for what she said was her fault, she had taken on many obsessions. She developed a terrible fear of water and would only go in a pool if there was a lifeguard present. She became super attentive to her surroundings. She raised money to help people who had less than she. Alexis was in a proverbial "guilt trap."

During our next session, Alexis talked more about what she wanted to accomplish in therapy. She wanted to take the journey from "guilt ridden" to "guilt riddance." She realized how guilt was paralyzing her. She had trouble with relationships because she was always second-guessing herself about whether she was making the right choices. Academically she did fine, although she would also second-guess whether or not she answered test questions correctly.

I explained to Alexis what I thought was happening. Alexis was over-compensating for the loss of Brian and the subsequent guilt she felt about falling asleep when she was supposed to be watching him. Over-compensation is what guilt-ridden people do to assuage their feelings of guilt. Indeed, many people develop obsessive-compulsive behaviors and rituals in response to guilt feelings. In Alexis' case, she felt the need to make the world a better place and make sure that everyone was safe and protected. When I explained this concept to Alexis, she nodded with understanding. "You see, Dr. Lasson, that was why I was so interested in the bystander effect. I have been plagued by these feelings of guilt. After your class I decided to revisit Brian's death, but I did not feel like anybody could really understand what I was going through."

Alexis made tremendous progress. She was open to new ways of thinking and divorced herself from the black and white, hero or zero style of thinking that many obsessive people engage in. She recognized how feeling guilty was paralyzing her from moving on with her life. Her level of insight was phenomenal and her commitment to her therapy was inspiring.

After we terminated our face-to-face sessions, Alexis continued to keep up with me from time to time, sharing the highlights of her life. She hosted a celebration of life commemorating the tenth year since Brian's passing and reread the poem she had written years before. Alexis continues to inspire others and support those grieving the loss of a loved one. It is individuals like Alexis who inspire me to continue the work that I do.

I Don't Like
Happy Therapists

Too many people spend money they haven't earned, to buy things they don't want, to impress people they don't like.
—Will Smith

One of the joys of working in a practice with other therapists is the opportunity to converse with one another during coffee break, over lunch, or during group supervision and share your feelings about your clients' progress—or lack thereof.

Any honest therapist will tell you that not all clients are likable. I personally struggle with narcissistic clients. It is challenging to show them the unconditional positive regard that is fundamental to the therapeutic relationship. The personal hurt I have felt working with narcissists and other populations is an ongoing struggle, but it is *my* struggle, not the clients'. As therapists we have to be careful to make that delineation. If you don't like working with older adults, for example, that is *your* problem and not the problem of the elderly person who has come for help. As a competent therapist, you must address your feelings. Indeed, counter-transference issues arise where the therapist cannot overcome their animosity toward a specific population.

Psychology, like philosophy or archaeology, involves digging. Philosophers dig for answers to existential issues and psychologists dig for answers to problems of the human psyche. Some archaeologists may have interest in ancient pottery, while others prefer to look for ruins of old cities. Likewise, teachers have favorite students. Why wouldn't they? Everyone has a particular niche they really enjoy, and psychologists are far from the exception. I once read that in mental health we are, in a sense, working with our autobiographies. We choose a theoretical orientation that best suits our worldview. Sure, we'd like to work only with the clients we enjoy and pawn off the others to colleagues, but it doesn't always work that way.

One of my colleagues, Cindy, a wonderful person and skilled therapist, called me over during a lunch break and told me that she would no longer be seeing Vince. Vince was a twenty-four-year-old college student who suffered from bipolar depression. They had gotten to a therapeutic stalemate, and it was mutually agreed that Vince needed to be transferred to a different therapist. She shared her session notes, and I said I would see him.

The first meeting it became clear: Vince was not a very likable fellow. From the start, I wondered why Cindy chose me as the most suitable therapist. She knew that I struggled with narcissistic people and Vince would put Narcissus himself to shame. (I began plotting my revenge on Cindy, thinking of difficult clients I might send her.)

Vince came in and presented as a handsome but somewhat awkward young man who appeared to be slightly older than his stated age. Immediately upon entering my office, he looked around and declared, "We are not meeting here." He looked at the couch and said, "That is filthy!" Although I hadn't chosen the decor of that office, I was taken aback. I do my best to keep my workspace clean. Nonetheless, I offered him my chair, which he gladly accepted. Then he assailed me with questions about my credentials. When I told him where I went to school he said, "Never heard of it." Then, noting my yarmulke he said, "A Jew. This should be fun." I let his remark go and decided to make a light-hearted attempt to process with him.

"Vince, I have not even begun to get to know you, and I see that you are already putting distance between the two of us. Is this typical for you, or are you just having a difficult day?"

Vince made an abysmal attempt to assuage the tension in the room. "I have not seen one of those since my first year in college," he said pointing to the yarmulke. "My economics professor wore one. I did not particularly enjoy the class but got an A anyway, without ever cracking open the book."

Silence.

"Are you offended by what I said?" Vince asked with a mischievous smirk. "Do you still have, what do they call that, unconditional positive regard for me?" he, seeming to have fun with the conversation.

In a therapeutic relationship, clients often put up a guard especially when they have severe trust issues. They will ether employ a defense mechanism, which Freud coined "intellectualization," or they will attempt humor or they might try to annoy the therapist to the point that it is unclear who is more unstable. Vince chose the latter technique. However, he was about to meet his match.

I chose my words carefully. "Vince, when you came in and I gave you my chair, what was your first thought about me?"

"You are weak. You are so desperate to try to fix me that you would have given me your shirt, too, although I would never wear something that looked like that." He smiled again awaiting my reaction.

Next tactic. "Vince, I understand that you have seen three of my colleagues so far in the past year. What are you here for?"

"Why don't you just read Cindy's notes? Or did you, and you just want me to tell you in my own words?" he asked again, obviously having fun goading me.

"Honestly, I meant to read them but did not have a chance." More silence. He scanned my face looking for more ammunition to feed his narcissism.

I have learned that in therapy, counselors must employ the golden rule of silence when they feel their own blood pressure begin to rise. I recognized what was going on, as I had dealt with individuals like Vince before, although never someone this extreme. Another rule that I have learned over time is always to keep a poker face. I keep my facial expressions in check even when clients tell me the most troubling stories.

Instead, I do my best to match their emotional states. Vince and I were playing a game of therapeutic chess.

"Why are you no longer meeting with Cindy?" I asked.

"I didn't care for her style. She would just repeat everything I said. Although she went to a more prestigious university than you did, you would never be able to tell. She probably would be better suited to working with children."

"Is that all?" I continued.

"She was also boring. I only stayed with her because I thought she was cute. The one thing that really bothered me about her was that she always seemed happy. I don't know what she smokes, but I don't like happy people, and I certainly don't like happy therapists. You don't look like a happy person, so I will give it a shot despite your mediocre education."

(If you're thinking homicidal thoughts about Vince right about now, I understand. Vince, as I mentioned, was not a likable person.)

"Well, I certainly thank you for giving me a chance to help you, I . . . "

Vince cut me off. "I wonder if you are capable of helping anyone. What is your success rate?"

I decided to play into his narcissism and flatter him with a slight untruth. "Not very high. You are very astute. Many of my clients see me as a sad person, as you mentioned, and they feel that I can't possibly help others if I myself am depressed. Others feel they can relate better to me because they understand that I have suffered my share of misery. Kind of like a recovering alcoholic working with individuals who are alcoholics."

Vince did not know what to make of this response. He was most probably expecting—or hoping—that I would become rattled and scream, "You nasty, vile creep! Get a life and get out of my office!"

(There had been a span in my life beginning at around age thirty where I began to suffer from debilitating migraine headaches. I probably had suffered from them for a longer period of time but never knew what they were, aside from excruciating. Thankfully, with the help of my neurologist and my own stress-reduction techniques, they are significantly more manageable nowadays. But, I feared that Vince was going to give me a mind-blowing migraine. Although I successfully maintained my poker face the entire session, I was stunned and could not imagine how Vince could ever improve given his resistance.)

Apparently, Vince finally decided I was "unhappy" enough to work with, and he told me why he was here: he'd just been fired from his fifth job in a year. Each employer, according to Vince, was dumber than the last. Vince boasted that he had graduated at the top of his class from a "prestigious" university. He rattled off tale after tale, without any emotion, of the different companies he had worked for and how they were all incompetent.

I did not say much, and frankly I did not hear much. I was still trying to figure out what to do with Vince. Thankfully, our session was just about over. "It was nice meeting you," I lied and did not bother asking him to see the receptionist to make another appointment.

The next day I bumped into Cindy in the break room. She smiled at me and asked how my first session with Vince had gone. I pointed my fingers at my head and pretended to shoot myself. "Great," I said. "I will never forgive you." Cindy apologized and admitted there was nothing more she could do for him and figured he might do better with a male therapist. Cindy was still smiling—the way she always did. . . . My head hurt.

I turned off the lights and lay down, thinking only about Vince. What made him think that I looked like a sad person? Was he right? My colleagues all think that I bring a breath of fresh air to the office with my quick wit and generous nature. I am a pretty happy guy, when I am not having a migraine. Then the questioning about my credentials. I was proud to some extent of how I handled Vince but was bothered by *why* I was so bothered.

Fortunately, the rest of the day went much better. I saw two more clients: Jarred, a very likable teenager who was struggling with the idea of coming out to his parents about his sexual orientation, and Cheryl, who came for hypnotherapy to relieve chronic pain. Two enjoyable clients to follow my newest nemesis.

The following week I was quite surprised when the receptionist put Vince on my schedule again. When I asked about it, she said that he had called and wanted to see me again. (I considered whether it might be a better idea to go to see my neurologist for that hour.)

Vince came in the next session, and I remained quiet. He looked at me and then looked at the couch. Seeing that I was not budging from my chair, he brushed off the couch and sat down. He asked whether I was ready to start. I looked back at him: "Go ahead."

"What do you want me to say?"

"I have no clue," I replied. "Usually I ask what brings you in today."

"Did you read the notes?" he asked.

"Yes, I read through them all," pretending to sound bored.

"So what do you think?" he asked, still with that smirk that I wanted to wipe off his face.

"Well, my credentials are no better than the other therapists that you have seen here, so I don't really know what I can offer that the others could not."

"Well you *are* different from the others," he countered.

"In what way?" I asked, thinking that maybe there would be a breakthrough.

"Well, for one, you're the first Jewish therapist I have ever seen and, number two, you're the first male therapist I have ever seen."

I responded, "So let's go with number two first. What about my being male do you think will make a difference in the therapy outcome for you?"

"I guess, a different perspective. The ladies that I saw . . . they were easy to play. I always liked choosing lady therapists because it gave me something to look at." He continued to smile as though he were enjoying this give and take. I certainly was not.

"And fantasize about?" I asked.

"Yeah, like any other guy," he responded, as if it were obvious. "Are you like any other guy?" I asked.

"I would think so. I am certainly not gay like that guy in the waiting room if you were wondering." I reminded myself that Vince was not a very likable person and that was precisely why he was here. I thought I was starting to get the upper hand in this game of chess.

"Last week you said that you stopped seeing Cindy because she was too happy. What if you saw a man that was happy? Would you like that person?"

"Well, that's why I made another appointment to see you. You seem the type that does not get overly emotional. I don't like emotional people. People need to get over things and chill out.

That's why I like Donald Trump. He says it like it is and does not care about political correctness. He transforms emotions into passion."

"That's a very interesting statement about transforming," I went back to paraphrasing and encouraging more from Vince. "Are you here to transform?" I asked.

"Obviously. I mean I already told you that I keep losing jobs. I want to be able to stay at one job, but those losers just don't like my political views and maybe my political incorrectness."

"So you agree that you need to change?"

"I guess. But not my viewpoints."

"So how do you propose to remain at a job if you have a recognized pattern of making reckless off-putting comments at work?" I asked, without emotion.

"Well, maybe I did not or do not always recognize that what I say is offensive."

"Can you see it now?"

"A little bit, but not worth losing a job over. I thought of suing the bastards."

Now we were taking a couple of steps back just when I thought I was making some progress. Vince decided that instead of making some changes in his approach and general attitude, he would shift the blame onto his employers. His sense of entitlement often got in the way of any possible progress. Just then, Vince got off the couch and began pacing back and forth in the cramped quarters of my office. I thought he was going to leave, but he sat back down, lost in thought.

"Vince, are you able to tell me what you are thinking right now?"

"Yeah, I am thinking how I am just too smart for some people and I need to find a company who would appreciate my knowledge."

(*Getting nowhere fast, Doc*, I whispered to myself.) "Do you think there is any way that I can help you?"

"Probably not."

"So would you like to terminate our sessions," I asked without batting an eyelash. "So soon? Let me think about it," was his response.

He walked out. My initial hope was that he would not come back because of his abrasive personality, but another part of me felt that I needed to get past *my* issue and do whatever I could to help him.

Later that day I thought about the famous Socratic quote: An unexamined life is not worth living. I would hate to think of a client's life as wasted, but for the moment I could not be of help to him. I did not think he was capable of seriously examining himself.

I consulted with Cindy. She laughed when I jokingly reminded her that I would never forgive her. We talked about Vince. She had a similar experience and came to the conclusion that he remained with her only because she was female and he enjoyed manipulating her. She played into the manipulations for as long as she could. At home she would cry, but in the office she pretended that everything was hunky dory. We agreed that Vince was a troubled soul.

I decided that if Vince chose to come back to see me that I would take a more aggressive approach. Part of that decision was due to the fact that he perceived me as weak, and I wanted to show him that I was not. However, I had to step back from that stance and remind myself that this was about him and not about me. I then rationalized that taking a tough approach might be the only shot I have to make any impression on Vince.

After two weeks, the office manager said that Vince wanted to come in for one last session with me. In a way, I was glad that this would be only a three-session case, but I was also curious as to why he wanted to see me again at all.

Vince came in to the session wearing his workout clothes, which looked as though they had just come from the dry cleaners. (I wondered to myself whether he dry-cleaned his underwear too, with heavy starch.) There was also a noticeable black and blue mark over his left eye. I was going to ask about it, but he volunteered.

"I guess you are wondering about the bruise." (*Wow, he is good*, I mused to myself. I was actually more interested in knowing why he decided to come back.)

"I met a woman at the gym who was gorgeous. I mean drop-dead, model-like gorgeous. It seemed like we hit it off right away. She must have been impressed by me because she commented on my intellect. She also liked that I had a nice car. The ladies like that you know." My mind wandered to my beat-up Honda Pilot sitting in front of the office.

"Anyway, I invited her for drinks at a bar after workout. She seemed really into me, and I asked her if she wanted to come back to my place. She was a little tipsy, and I started making the moves. We were kissing and stuff, and then all of a sudden she told me to get off. She was giving me mixed messages, and I got upset. I asked her if she only agreed to come back with me because I had a nice car, and that is when she whacked me." I did my best to suppress my smile. He continued, "I am not a believer in hitting women, so I just told her to get out of the car and find another way home."

"When I got back to my pad, I saw the ugly bruise and vowed not to go out with people like her. I never shared this with you Doc, but I don't really trust women very much."

My turn. "You say you don't trust women, yet you like to manipulate them and find them cute? Tell me more about that."

Finally, some reflection: "As an only child, my parents gave me everything I wanted—video games, cars, the best schools—everything. The one thing that they did not give me was the touchy-feely stuff. We lived in a wealthy neighborhood with very few kids my age. My dad was a workaholic doctor who I later learned had an affair with one of the women in his office when I was in elementary school. My mom was a hotshot lawyer who was never home. Who knows what she did all those hours? I never asked. I don't like my father very much, but I still use him when I need money or connections. I always liked my mother and wanted her to be more motherly, but that wasn't her style. I was basically raised by a nanny, Rosita, who cooked for the family and put me to sleep when I was younger.

"Rosita was from Honduras but spoke pretty good English. I was always bothered that so many people living here can't speak the language. I almost punched out an ATM machine when it gave an option for Spanish," he said laughing out loud.

"Anyway, this nanny was really my mother figure for many years. I would say that I loved her, and when I got old enough to realize my sexual feelings, I would try to sneak a peek at her when she was in the shower. One time she caught me and told me that it was not appropriate, but I didn't care. I thought she was cute, and I really wanted more from her, if you know what I mean. I think my father was fooling around with her too, but I can't prove it. It was sort of a Freudian thing but with a nanny. What do they call that bull that you guys came up with when you want to kill your father to get to your mother?"

"Oedipus complex?" I offered.

"Yeah, that. I remember that from the one psych course I took in college. That Freud guy. He was a weird dude. Anyway, I used to have dreams of my father dying from some terrible disease that caused him to become impotent so I would be able to have Rosita to myself. So maybe Freud wasn't that off. But then it occurred to me that I never felt these types of feelings toward my mother, although I wanted her to compliment me on my achievements.

"I remember at my graduation from college watching the other parents give big hugs to their graduating children. My mom gave me a hug but it was without any real feeling. My dad was mostly on his cell phone texting away throughout the ceremony. What a jerk!"

I remained silent, not sure if Vince wanted to continue talking. "So what do you think, Doc?"

"Do you really want to know?" I asked.

"Well, I already figured out my life and why I am having trouble keeping jobs. It's my parents' fault. So there is no sense having you tell me the same thing."

I was hoping that he would have a little more insight, something beyond blaming his parents, but that was wishful thinking.

"So what will you do differently now that you understand yourself so well?" I asked.

"I definitely will take it slower with the women," he said laughing.

"What about work?" I continued without smiling.

"I don't know. I guess I will call my dad and ask him to get me another job. Today he plays golf, but I'll ask him tomorrow."

So much for the insightful "gestalt-like" moment therapists dream that their clients will have.

When I reflect back on some of my most industrious clients, one word I would *not* associate them with is "entitled." They often felt the opposite, that they were not worthy of anything good happening in their lives. Such people are capable of recognizing their erroneous and negative thinking and can subsequently rid themselves of destructive patterns of thought. All it takes is awareness. At this point, Vince lacked awareness.

"So I guess that's it, Doc. You've been a good sport," he said, patting me on the back of my shirt—that I had just bought at Target, on sale.

As Vince left, I wished him luck. I never saw him again.

Not all stories have happy endings. I was hoping that I would be able to help Vince. In a way, perhaps I did. I think he was entertained by therapy and used it for his self-serving needs. So if entertaining our clients for an hour is helpful, then I succeeded. If my purpose was to help Vince make some serious changes in his life, I failed miserably.

I've often wondered why I've had a difficult time dealing with narcissists. Much has to do with my personality, in general, plus the fact that I am not a very materialistic person. I don't value "things" per se. I value people, not their image. One of the ideas that I learned from studying Talmud is that when our time on this earth is over, we do not take anything with us. So why accumulate possessions? Of what value is it to us in the grand scheme of things?

This truth was borne out by the kids at a summer camp I used to work at. Whenever we went on a big trip, for example, to an amusement park, many campers would come back grumpy that they did not get to go on this or that ride or they didn't win anything in the arcade games. But at the end of the summer, when I asked them what their favorite thing they did all summer was, the answer was usually hiking through the hills or walking through streams. Their best memories came from experiences they shared, not things they acquired.

In a sense, I felt bad for Vince. I was sorry that he was never given such opportunities to appreciate the simple pleasures in life. Perhaps one day he would have an epiphany. The best I could do was just to play the role Vince was ready for at this point in his life.

I didn't allow myself to ruminate about Vince too long. Instead, I drove home in my beat-up Honda and gave my five-year-old daughter a big hug.

THE OLD WARRIOR

Wrinkles merely mark where smiles have been.
—Mark Twain

Every once in a while I have the privilege of working
with a client whose motivation impresses me. Usually,
the motivated ones are younger clients willing to make
changes to improve their lives or break old unproductive patterns. It is rare that I see someone in their eighties with such
motivation. Farjad was one of those rare exceptions.

The office manager handed me the intake form for Farjad.
It listed him as eight-four years old and suffering from chronic
pain. His list of medications was so long that I gave up reading
it after a minute. I could get to that another time.

Farjad looked to be his stated age but had an air of deter-
mination and resolve about him that was attractive and youth-
ful. He was well-groomed and over six feet tall, but he
hunched over his walker to navigate the halls to my office. I
offered to meet him in a room closer to the waiting room,

where his wife sat reading a book. He declined but asked if I could get his water bottle from her. She whispered to me that he had been to so many doctors for his pain. She dared me to say, "Your husband has chronic pain. Here is some Percocet." I assured her that I would not and could not offer that to her husband. After all, I was not a psychiatrist.

It hurt me to see an elderly man in so much pain. He had worked as an electrical engineer for over fifty years. The intense work out in the field had taken its toll. Farjad had suffered three heart attacks and undergone multiple surgeries, including the replacement of both knees and hips. He was taking all of his prescribed medications, which his wife dutifully put together for him in little Walgreens bags. Although Farjad was born in Iran, he did not have the slightest accent.

He spoke articulate English and seemed well-versed in many subjects, ranging from politics to engineering to history.

Farjad started our session by motioning to the waiting area. "You saw that woman out there who claims to be my wife?" I smiled noting his sense of humor. "She is an absolute saint. I don't know how the hell she puts up with me. All I do is get shuttled from doctor to doctor while she fills my baggies with pills and listens to me complain about how much pain I am in. She is the love of my life. A smart one, too, even though she never went to college."

"So how did you find me, Farjad?" I was curious to know.

"A woman at a doctor's office referred me to you. She said you had success with "people like me," he replied.

"People like you?" I asked.

"Yeah, people who are a chronic pain," he smiled and then we both laughed.

"You mean people who are *in* chronic pain," I corrected making sure I understood his humor correctly.

"Of course. I was just joking. Joking around helps me a little, but mostly I sit at home and try my best to keep occupied. Doesn't always work, Doc." He looked up and stared deeply into my eyes.

I continued, trying to avoid his gaze. "I noticed that you are on many medications and that you have endured many health challenges in your life. What would you say is your ideal goal for therapy?"

At times, clients will become sidetracked when discussing their story. I wanted to keep Farjad focused but soon came to realize that Farjad was full of wisdom even when sidetracked. He would often take a moment to linger over something that was said or a feeling that came over him. I came to appreciate those delays in his responses.

"I would like to be as pain-free as I can to relieve the burden I impose on Parva every day. She deserves a better life."

"So you are doing this more for your wife than for yourself?" He nodded and said, "I have not been able to give her much lately. Time. Love. Help with house chores. St. Francis once said, 'For it is in giving that we receive'. If I give, I will eventually receive. So in a sense you are right, Doctor. It is more for her at this time."

"Well, I will do my best to get you to a better physical state," I said, trying to sound confident. Working with people at this age was a challenge but there was something enticing about working with this "old warrior."

Looking at him, I questioned whether I was giving him false hope, but I had already committed myself. He had been told he had osteoarthritis, which could have resulted from his years as an engineer. The symptoms seemed to intensify later in the day or during times when he was not active. I explained that some of what I do would incorporate hypnotherapy techniques that have been found to be useful in alleviating chronic pain, especially back pain, which is where he experienced the majority of his symptoms. Farjad acknowledged he had never had hypnotherapy and was somewhat skeptical. I explained that the more motivated he was, the better the result. He was willing to give it his all.

I obtained a more detailed history from Farjad, who then requested that Parva join the session to fill in the blank areas he could not recollect. The two of them complemented each other very well, and it was quite evident that they shared a deep sense of respect and love for one another. As the first session came to a close, I gave Farjad some reading material on hypnotherapy and asked him to familiarize himself with this modality so that he would be more comfortable going into the next session.

Farjad and Parva came in the next week for his first therapy session. I informed Farjad that I would be dimming the lights and playing some soft music in the background. I asked that he let me know if he was uncomfortable with the music or the chair. In this particular office, which was further away from the noise of the secretary and office manager, we had a very comfortable reclining chair and a nice couch. I was hesitant to put him in the chair out of a fear that it would be too hard for him to get up from it once he'd sat down, so I asked him to sit on the couch. But he looked at the chair and said, "That looks more comfortable."

I helped ease him into the chair and reclined it until he was comfortable. He grimaced at times but did not express his pain outwardly. I admired his fighting spirit. I clicked on the music and began the initial induction phase with some deep breathing and muscle relaxation exercises. After about five minutes, Farjad was sound asleep. Not the result I was looking for, yet I wanted to let him rest. As our time was nearing its end, I woke him. He asked, "Did I fall asleep?"

"You most certainly did," I replied with a smile.

"Well, it felt good to nap like that, and by the way, you have a very soothing voice."

I thanked him and assured him that I was happy that he was able to sleep so comfortably. I helped him to his walker. On the way out he asked if he could record the next session. This was not an odd request; many other clients have asked the same. I assured him that would be fine.

When he came back the following week, he had his recorder with him but admitted he didn't know how to use it. I helped him get it set up, and we began again. He said that he experienced lots of pain mostly toward the end of the day, which for him was the late afternoon.

I assisted him in getting to a comfortable position in the chair, and we began again. This time, he remained somewhat conscious or as some would put it, in an "altered state of consciousness." I made several suggestions during the session about how to re-experience the way he conceptualized pain. When there were only fifteen minutes left of our session, he fell asleep again.

He asked me whether he could try to get up on his own from the chair. I conceded. He gave a slight grimace, and then with just two attempts he stood erect and smiled at his accomplishment. "Where do you get that music from? It's really nice." I like Native American music, and he apparently found it soothing as well. I told him where he could purchase the CD. He asked, "What's a CD?" and smiled again. "Just kidding!"

It is funny to see how elderly people perceive the younger generation of doctors. I truly believe that his sense of humor and the backing of his wife had kept him going thus far. With his new recording in hand, he proceeded with his walker down the hallway. His wife noticed him standing taller than usual, smiled at him, and said, "You are looking very handsome my dear. Taller then you were an hour ago." They gave each other loving smiles as she helped him to the car. I could not help but think of what I would be like at age eighty-four. I was in awe of Farjad and the beautiful relationship he had cultivated with his wife.

The next session, Farjad came in and said, "Doctor Lasson, I am no longer taking the Percocet and am weaning myself off some of the other medications." I checked whether he had consulted with his physician, and he said he had. I asked him to sign a release for me to speak with his physician, and he readily agreed.

The next few sessions went extremely well. In fact, so well that Farjad had stopped using his walker. He took his time while walking to and from my office. Everyone waved to him and knew him by name, as he was quite gregarious with others. He was now a friendly face in the office. The other therapists all admired him and commented how charming it was to see an older couple so much in love with each other.

I placed a call to his physician who confirmed that he had noticed an improvement in Farjad. He had been hesitant to reduce the medications, but Farjad was very insistent. I promised the physician that I would keep him posted if I felt something should be changed.

After about the twelfth session, Farjad reported that he was sleeping better and was getting back to some of the enjoyable activities that he used to engage in. He had a workshop in the basement where he liked to tinker with old radios, taking them apart and putting them back together. He was always careful when going down to the basement, and now that he no longer needed his walker, he had an easier time. He was so motivated that he was almost as quick as I was in getting from the waiting room to my office. Our latest game was to race to see who could get there faster. I took one route and he took another. Lately the race was ending in a tie. (Note to self: Get back to the gym!)

Farjad's recovery from chronic pain was certainly an outlier given his age, yet his progress was unequivocal. We decided to see each other every other week.

One week he came in wearing a sling on his arm. He noticed me looking at it and said, "Don't worry. I'm okay." I asked what had happened. He shared with me that while in his basement he'd overextended himself trying to reach a tool on a high shelf. He fell off the ladder and sprained his wrist. At the hospital they told him it was a bad sprain and he should not use the arm for at least eight weeks. I said sincerely, "I am so sorry." I exchanged a glance with Farjad as he adjusted his sling and wondered whether this would be a lifelong setback.

Farjad placed a bottle of Percocet in front of me. I was not sure what his intention was, but it reminded me of the number of clients I had who abused pain medication. I vowed to help people reduce their dependency on pain medicine. "They also gave me this," pointing to the bottle. "I told them there was no way I was taking it. The doctor asked me how I was going to handle the pain. I told him that I am going to Doctor Lasson." We both smiled. "I told the doctor at the hospital that I bet I will recover quicker than most people. Hospitals are for sick people." Indeed, Farjad was right.

The power of the mind is amazing. Farjad had so much going for him—a loving wife, a loving family and the motivation of an old warrior in battle with chronic pain.

AM I ON *THE WIRE*?

You can have it all, just not all at once.
—Oprah Winfrey

During the year that I worked at Fillmore Middle School, I also counseled students at a small elementary school located directly behind it, called Wilbur Wilson. This school was the Taj Mahal compared to Fillmore Middle School. I had a huge office—not that it mattered, because I was so busy with His Individualized Education Plan (IEP) meetings and classroom observations that I never really got to use it.

Two wonderful human beings ran the show at Wilbur Wilson: Ms. Elma Jones and Mr. Cortez Jones (no relation). There was a sense of order at the school, and it was maintained nicely. I enjoyed working with the younger children. Elementary school students in the inner city are usually more plugged in than middle school students. Plus, there is slightly more parental involvement, which made the work interesting.

The impression of the inner city from outsiders is mostly formed by news or viewing episodes of *The Wire*. I was working in neighborhoods that looked identical to scenes on TV. Even the characters on the street looked familiar. I would swear I saw *Bubbles* or *Bunk Moreland*—or at least their look-alikes.

To this point I had been unaware of the level of poverty and violence that plagued the community surrounding Johns Hopkins Hospital. Aside from my weekly coffee runs to Hopkins, I rarely walked around the neighborhood. However, as a school psychologist who was also charged with IEP development and implementation, there were times I had to go to a child's home for the simple purpose of obtaining signatures from a parent. Many parents could not attend meetings because they didn't have child care or were incarcerated or for some host of other reasons that kept parents indoors.

One morning, I set out to get a signature from a parent when Mr. Jones asked me where I was heading. "You can't go to that home," he said. I asked why not. "It's in a project in one of the most dangerous neighborhoods on the East Side," he explained. I insisted. Besides I wanted to see what the projects were really like. I was young and naïve. Mr. Jones said, "I'll come with you. It's not safe to go alone. If parents see a white dude coming, they won't talk to you. They'll think you are coming to arrest them or take away their kids. And it's best not to make too much eye contact with anyone." I got the point and decided to lay low.

We headed to the home of Kiara, a second-grader whose mother could not attend her IEP meeting held earlier that day.

Mr. Jones turned to me and said, "Doc, take a good look at the outside of this home." Some windows were boarded up while others had bullet holes in them. "This is what many of our students see on a daily basis."

We headed up the stairs, lined with young men hanging out and smoking weed. We knocked on Kiara's door. A young man answered. Mr. Jones stated who we were and the purpose of our visit. The young man reluctantly opened the door and screamed out a woman's name. I noticed Kiara lying on the couch under a very dirty blanket, drinking orange soda, and watching television. The young man looked over at Kiara and back at us. "She ain't feeling good today, so she didn't go to school."

I had only met Kiara once but remembered her very well. She was born with fetal alcohol syndrome, which was evident in her facial features. She had an anxious look on her face as though something bad was going to happen. I assured her that we were just coming to talk to her mother.

Finally, her mother came out from behind the door of a closed room. We reminded her about Kiara's IEP meeting, but she didn't seem to care and just asked where to sign. I looked over at Kiara's sad expression, smiled at her, and said, "I hope you feel better and come back to school soon." She smiled back at me and waved goodbye. We left the home and quickly headed back to school. On our way back, Mr. Jones told me that Kiara's mother was known to sell her body for drugs and that the community had a rampant HIV and violence problem. I was taking notes, feeling overwhelmed with pity for this family and the situation they were in.

Inner-city life affords outsiders like myself the ability to get a better glimpse into the awful predicament that impacts so many people. The schools are given the tremendous responsibility of trying to educate students, whom many have given up on. The parents are faced with societal pressures, namely a drug culture, rampant prostitution, and sickness. To survive in the inner city takes a certain level of street smarts, but also educational reform.

Much of the educational reform that has been proposed simply does not work. Throwing money toward programs that can only work with parental involvement has proven to be a fruitless endeavor. Many school psychologists who were educated in new techniques of reaching students in low socioeconomic neighborhoods end up abandoning what they learned in graduate school, realizing that what may work in more privileged neighborhoods doesn't work when you don't have parental involvement.

I can attest to the difference. In the schools my own children attend, 90 to 95 percent of the parents show up for conferences, whereas in the inner city, you are lucky to see 10 percent show up. It is a sad statement, and it invigorates idealists like me to want to do something about it.

During that year, many social work interns were sent to the school to help address another major issue—attendance. They ran reports and had meetings, ran more reports and had more meetings to discuss those reports, and some more meetings to discuss what went on at those meetings. I thought these interns could have been put to better use. But I was just a school psychologist, and most of what I said was overruled simply because it was suggested by me. So from that point onward, when I had a suggestion, I gave it over to a veteran who suggested it to the principal, and the idea was subsequently implemented. I learned that oppositional defiant behaviors exist not only in children but in school administrators as well.

Not only is lack of parental participation and irregular attendance challenging, but the relationship between the police departments and the community complicates the picture even more. Schools situated in more affluent areas will rarely see police activity, let alone a police car. Police cars at Baltimore City public schools are such a common sight that people do not pay attention to them.

I had never seen inside of a police car until I worked at a school with a program for students identified as emotionally disturbed. These students were frequently transported to University of Maryland Hospital when it was determined that they were a danger to themselves or others. The principal was convinced that as the school psychologist, I was one of the only people around who could ask for an emergency petition to have Baltimore's finest transport an emotionally disturbed student to the hospital. I probably spent more time in the Pediatric ER than I spent in the school itself. (This was okay because leaving the school frequently meant freedom from an environment that had more toxins embedded in its walls than Three Mile Island!)

This school had sent its share of children with severe behavioral issues to the ER. Derrick, at the tender age of nine, was one such student. Derrick was not a very communicative child but he did have a knack for artistic expression. Most of his artwork was morbid and consisted of guns pointing at police officers with blood squirting out of every possible orifice. Some of his anger-based drawings were self-directed. He had been hospitalized on several occasions for threatening to kill himself by walking into oncoming traffic and trying to jump out of third-story windows.

I remember when another suicidal student was screaming that he wanted to die. I ran upstairs arriving just in time to see him dive head first out the window. I instinctively grabbed him and yanked him back inside. He landed on me, which led to two unsuccessful surgeries on my left hand. I am, to this day, unable to use my left index finger to play ball or my treasured saxophone.

One day, I was called to the classroom where Derrick was hitting his head on the ground. His teacher, a wonderful young lady who worked very hard to contain these children, had him placed in a basket hold, which is part of the training you receive about how to work with this population. She asked if I could EP (emergency petition) him to the hospital. After determining that Derrick was in fact a danger to himself and possibly others, I filled out the papers for the EP.

In the meantime, the school attempted to contact his mother. She did not want to be bothered by another visit to the school, but the administrator insisted that if she did not come down, Derrick would not be able to remain in the program. The school police and I waited for the mother for a couple hours as Derrick thrashed and kicked in an attempt to get away. Finally, another officer was sent to pick up the mother and bring her to the school. Upon seeing her son, she said "I ain't goin' to no hospital with him."

"Let him go," she said, pointing at me.

The officer looked at the mother sternly and said, "I am telling you this as a black brother to a black sister. Dr. Lasson did not make this child. It's not his responsibility to take care of him. Now you get your sorry (expletive) down to that (expletive) hospital and take care of your own child."

I was spared a ride in the police car that day. However, my encounters with law enforcement were not limited to my transports of emotionally disturbed students to area hospitals.

I am someone who has never smoked, experimented with drugs, or engaged in other high-risk behavior. It's not that I have not been offered these opportunities, it's just that I've seen the terrible effects on individuals and their families. So when I was accused of drug possession by a police officer, I almost burst out laughing.

The incident took place at the corner of two, crime-ridden streets on the west side of the city. The surrounding neighborhood was a smattering of projects, boarded up homes, and drug dealers on most every street corner. One day, as I came to a stop at Wilbur Wilson Elementary, where I worked as a school psychologist, I noticed two police cars right behind me with their lights on. I followed the "Police Stop Best Practices Manual" (which, of course, does not really exist) and kept both hands on the wheel and waited for further instructions. The policewoman rapped on my window and told me to get out of the car and put my hands on the hood. I complied, as she patted me down. She seemed satisfied that I was not carrying any weapons. I innocently asked if everything was okay. She, in turn, asked, "What are you doing here?"

By this time some of the students, including two who were on my caseload, were coming into the school building. They found it funny to see the school psychologist with his hands on the hood. I responded to the officer that I worked at the school. She persisted, "Let me see your school ID."

"I don't carry ID," I replied. She then began to search me again. The kids loved this.

I politely asked her if that, instead of a second pat down, she would come with me into the building to verify that I indeed worked there. I also begged her not to put the cuffs on. By this time a few other officers came for backup, so she acquiesced to my request. We entered the main office.

"We found this man outside the building, and he claims to work here," the policewoman said.

The principal, who enjoyed a good laugh, looked at me and the officer and said, "Never seen him before. He's probably here for drugs!"

My heart almost came out of my chest until she said, "Just kidding. Doc is with us." As I went back to my car to retrieve my workbag, I noticed a bumper sticker on a car that read, "I Love City Life." I almost kicked that car, but I probably would have been arrested for vandalism. At that moment, city life and I were not feeling the love.

Crisis intervention is a large part of the job of a school psychologist. We never know when we will be called. Just as paramedics and other first responders, we are always prepared—somewhat.

One year, I was placed in one of the most violent schools I had seen in my years as a school psychologist. The high school was home to the Bloods and Crypts. Fights broke out every day, and even the school security was ill equipped to deal with the tumult at this school. The metal detectors at the front of the building were of no use: the students had dismantled them a long time ago. There was some checking of people's bags when they entered the building, but it was not very thorough.

I remember meeting the principal of the school and while talking to him, a student was slammed into the lockers not two feet away from where we were standing. The principal did not say or do anything. He just turned to me and said, "They are so playful." I don't think he lasted long.

That year, I was tasked with supervising an intern from a local University. She would occasionally shadow me at some of the schools that I served. One day, she and I heard a lot of commotion in the hallway. We went out to see what was going on. It turned out that one of the security guards was being pummeled by a couple of students much to the delight of the gathering crowd. I told her to follow me and stay low to the ground because things were about to get ugly. We rushed into the main office where the secretary quickly shut the door behind us. At that point about 40 police officers stormed the building with guns drawn. I have never been so frightened. They finally dispersed the crowd and took the security guard to the hospital for treatment.

Another day, we heard about a student at another school who had been killed on school grounds. Crisis counselors were deployed to the school. Since I was on the crisis team, I thought it would be a good idea to bring along my intern to show her how it works. When I knocked on the classroom's door, the teacher gave us the stare-down. In front of the students, she asked why we were there. We explained, and she sighed to the students, "Okay, even though these people are not from our community, they have come to talk to you about what happened in school yesterday." I thanked her for her "warm" introduction and went ahead and passed out paper for the students to draw pictures or write about their feelings. We proceeded to talk to the children and put to use the skills that we had honed over the years to help them express their feelings about the young man who died too young. My intern and I were stunned. We'd never been treated this way by a teacher before. Fortunately, some teachers welcomed our intervention.

Norton High School was one of the largest high schools in the city with well over 2,400 students. It had its share of violent days as well. One such day involved a gang-related shooting that left one student dead near the school. Again, the crisis team was deployed. I went to a twelfth-grade class where the students were already sitting in a circle awaiting my arrival. The teacher was a kind woman who was equally shaken by the student's death. She first had all the students hold hands in the circle and share a thought or memory about him. The students talked about how kind he was and how he would always make everyone laugh. Apparently, he had been quite popular at the school.

I began by offering my condolences to the class and validating their pain. We talked about how everyone grieves in their own way. "If you don't see someone crying, it does not mean they are not upset at the loss," I explained. One young lady in the circle fought back tears and said that she knew that she would not live past twenty-five because of the violence that surrounded her. Each student then predicted how long they would live, and not one student thought that they would live past thirty. How sad to hear students in the prime of life thinking about their premature deaths. Seeing my bewildered expression after that discussion, one young lady turned to me and said, "I am sure you are a nice person and all, but you have no idea what we go through. I am sure you live in a rich neighborhood where it's safe to walk in the streets. You don't know what it's like to have to lay on the floor every night to avoid being sprayed by gunfire." I thought back to Kiara's home near Johns Hopkins. She was right. I could never truly understand what these kids had to live through every day.

I cannot predict the future. The plight of inner-city youth remains a moving target. As school psychologists, we face pressure to help students get through the system. I have seen many school psychologists move to other jurisdictions where there is more parental involvement, while others stay because they understand that success is not dependent on the number of students you helped but how much effort you put into the child, regardless of the outcome.

In life, people come and go. In the inner city, students move around, and many do not survive. I refuse to become callous toward their plight, despite what others might do. Each student is a diamond in the rough waiting for someone to let them shine. My personality causes me to become attached to the people whom I work with, and my personality also causes me to feel guilty when I fail in getting through and uncovering these diamonds.

There are other factors that are a cause for reflection aside from my self-imposed guilt: societal norms and school systems that are over-regulated in order to free themselves from consent decrees,

My goal is to bring awareness and let other competent people bring about reform. As individuals, we have to remain vigilant and help our inner-city youth in order to foster hope for survival.

YOU'RE A RACIST!

In order to love yourself, you must behave in ways that you admire. —Irvin D. Yalom

Dealing with members of a tight-knit religious community can pose several challenges. I frequently tell people, in jest, that the difference between my non-religious and religious clients is that my non-religious clients come on time, pay on time, and never say, "I'll see you in synagogue tonight." Of course, that is not always the case, but it does illustrate the potential dual conflicts that might occur.

One of my rabbis, upon hearing that I was entering the mental health profession, told me that there is a great need in our religious community for more psychologists who know what they are doing. He wanted to make sure that our close community would be my primary focus.

I think back to that conversation that took place over twenty-five years ago with mixed feelings. On the one hand, I feel that working with those who share my religion helps people relate better and saves lots of wasted time trying to understand another culture. On the other hand, becoming entrenched in the community where you are bound to cross paths with your clients can be very awkward and challenging. We see each other at Bar Mitzvah celebrations, weddings, funerals, or simply walking down the street. I usually process this with my religious clients during our first session and advise them on how to act if they see me outside of the office.

Another mentor of mine, who was a psychologist-turned-rabbi, warned me early on that psychology is a very lonely profession. He explained that we generally see and interact with very few people outside of work on a daily basis, especially if you are in private practice. We can't share our frustrations or even our inspiring tales with family members. Others do not like to be seen with us because people will assume if you are talking to a psychologist, you are either a client or a potential client. He was absolutely right about the loneliness aspect. I come home after a day's work with no one to talk to about my day. If my wife asks me how my day was, I can't tell her it was stressful because Yossi is suicidal and Yankel is back in rehab. I just have to come home and be cheerful and pretend that nothing out of the ordinary happened that day.

But when you are a mental health clinician, something out of the ordinary happens practically every day.

My wife always tells her friends that her husband is so confidential and she does not know what goes on in my practice. I would hope that most professionals are like that. I told her that she would be surprised at some of the stories she will eventually read in this book because I have never shared them with my family. My professional life is private, and so are the lives of my clients. It is an understanding she has come to learn over the years, as have my children.

There are times when members of the religious community where I live will come over to my wife and even to my children and say, "Your husband (or your father) was my psychologist" or "Your husband really helped my son." I cannot control what people say to my family members, but it is awkward for me even though it might not be awkward for my clients.

Avi, a twenty-two-year-old student in a local *yeshiva* (rabbinic seminary) came to me after taking my Introduction to Psychology class a couple of years back. He told me that he was having issues with dating. In the Orthodox world, young men are paired up with suitable mates by someone called a *shadchan,* or a matchmaker in English. The *shadchan* has lists of eligible young men and women with profiles and sometimes pictures that they show to interested parents and those dating when they inquire. (For a better understanding of the dating process in the Orthodox Jewish world, although it is less dramatic in real life, I would recommend watching the film *Arranged*.)

When Avi came in for his first scheduled session, he was about fifteen minutes late. I did not recognize him, but that was nothing new for me as I am notoriously bad with faces. I informed him that we would not be able to have a full session as I had another client immediately afterward. He sat down and got straight to the point. "You know, I have dated almost twenty girls and they all seem to say *no* to me after one or two dates. What's my problem?"

Wow! He was not interested in small talk. I was curious to know what he felt was the problem and was tempted to go that route but decided to inquire more about the dates.

"What do you typically do on your first date?" I asked.

"We usually go to a hotel lobby and talk. Sometimes I bring a game and ask her if she wants to play something like Taboo or Bananagrams. I usually end up talking politics because that is what I really like to talk about. This country is run by very stupid politicians, so I often explain to the girls a little about politics. They are usually clueless. Most of them couldn't even tell me the name of the vice president. Maybe I am just too smart for these girls," he suggested. (Many thoughts were swirling through my mind when he made this comment.)

Sometimes in therapy, employing a humanistic approach works very well, and I usually prefer that modality over a more directive approach. Avi was a different story. If I were to ask him how dating made him feel or inquire about his unconscious inner conflicts, it would probably end up backfiring. Some people just need common sense knocked into them, the good old-fashioned way.

As Avi was talking about how dumb the girls he dated were, memories of Avi sitting in my class started to come back to me. I recalled some of the obnoxious and often racist comments he would make when discussing minorities. He would always look around the class to see whether anyone was laughing at his remarks. Thankfully, my students, for the most part, were respectful of other cultures and did not give him the pleasure of responding to his rude comments. One student even complained to me that I should not let him speak in class because he was such an offensive person. I kept this in mind when I decided to be blunt with him.

"Avi, I think I know what your problem is and why you get turned down so often. However, I am hesitant to tell you because I don't want to be so blunt," I said tentatively.

"I'm from New York, Doc, so I can handle it," was his response. "Do you really want to know?" I asked.

"Of course! That's why I am paying you," he replied.

I said, "Okay, but this is not my usual style." Pausing and clearing my throat, I said in a loud tone, "YOU'RE A RACIST!" This was very surprising for Avi to hear coming from this generally soft-spoken therapist.

I waited for his response. He was somewhat surprised by the change in my demeanor, which was mostly an act. I repeated myself again, even louder this time: "YOU'RE A RACIST!" Avi seemed a little confused, but he was used to this abrupt manner of speech—after all, he was a New Yorker.

"So what? I know lots of people who are married and share my view on things," he explained, "especially with regard to politics. You know that Nancy Pelosi is such a . . ." I did not let him finish his thought.

I moved closer to Avi and said, in a quieter tone now, "Avi, listen to me. You came here because you are being rejected left and right by young women whom you are seeking out as potential marriage partners. I am going to go out on a limb here and make an assumption about you. If you are a racist, you are probably also a sexist."

He asked for clarification. "People with extreme views about minorities like yourself tend to view women as a minority as well. That might be what is becoming very evident to these young women early on in your dates. I remember you now from the class you took with me. In that class, you made many hate-filled, racist comments. I did not feel it necessary to correct you at the time, which, in hindsight, I probably should have. But now you are seeking my help."

"So what do I do?" he asked.

"Well first, you must disavow yourself of these hateful thoughts. Second, you must realize that most people, especially those you are considering for marriage, do not care for cynicism or racism and they certainly would not care for sexist comments like the one you made earlier today." I reminded him of the comment about how dumb girls can be. He nodded.

Our hour was almost over, so I suggested that he try to come a little earlier next time so we can have a full session.

The next session, Avi came on time. He had a look of defeat on his face. He sat down but seemed more guarded and waited for me to begin.

"Avi, I apologize if I was a bit harsh with you last session. Much of what I said was based on my impressions of you from class. When you came for therapy, I realized that others probably shared my impressions as evidenced by your dating woes."

He looked up at me and said, "You know, Doc, you are the first person who ever hit me over the head like that. You tell it like it is, and I think that is what I needed. But how do I change? I'm bound to mess up again."

"Avi, I am sure you will mess up again, but now you know what to look out for, and when you do mess up you should immediately apologize. You won't lose your man card by apologizing for things that you say.

"The next thing you need to do is learn to be culturally sensitive. You will encounter many people over the years whom you have made jokes about in the past. As you see, poking fun at minorities and women whom you perceived as inferior has gotten you nowhere. You are way too young to use the motto that 'you can't teach an old dog new tricks'. You can change; I am confident about that." I was taking a risk here, because, in reality, I was not very confident about his ability to change at the time. But he was a captive audience in my theater, so I used my artistic license to continue the act.

Avi then told about how his father was very similar and made racist jokes all the time. When asked how he treated his mother, he looked down. "I guess I did not have the greatest role models in life. My father would sit at the Shabbat table and basically be served. When he talked, he expected everyone else to listen. He would always tell off-color jokes, which at the time I thought were funny." He sat in thoughtful silence for a bit and then got up, looking exhausted.

Over the next few sessions we role-played what to say and what not to say on a date and how to listen better. Avi worked on changing his worldview, especially his attitude toward women. After a couple of months of therapy, Avi announced that he was going to Israel for a year to study. I did not hear from him for a couple of years after that until an invitation to his wedding came to my office. Apparently, Avi had met a young lady with whom he wanted to spend the rest of his life. There was a personal note attached to the invitation that read: "Thanks, Doc, for changing my worldview. I could not have done it without you giving me that kick in the pants. Hope you can be there."

There are many people out there who are not very pleasant to be around—which is part of the reason they end up in therapy. In this day and age, there are so many opportunities to learn about multiculturalism and diversity. In order to become an effective clinician and a competent, sensitive human, for that matter, multicultural sensitivity is essential.

When I think back to Avi, I realize that growing up in a home where racism and sexism are repudiated, like the home I am thankful to have grown up in, children will learn and act accordingly. The same is true if the opposite experience occurs. We must be so careful about the words we use around our children and how we speak of other cultures. Some children will reject the racist and sexist views they hear, while others will see these comments as the norm.

Avi was an extreme for me. By extreme, I mean that he had become very narrow-minded in his way of thinking. Most Orthodox Jewish clients whom I have dealt with, are extremely respectful toward others and go out of their way to learn to become culturally sensitive. Many non-religious colleagues of mine have commented along the same line.

Although many religious people live in self-contained and insulated communities, it is a misnomer to make a blanket assumption and label them as intolerant of others.

Avi was an interesting case for me in that I departed from my traditional person-centered approach to therapy. I understood the need to alter things a bit, mostly because many clients cannot afford long-term therapy, but also flexibility is necessary because some people just don't adapt well to a humanistic approach. I learned that sometimes I need to be a little "unorthodox" when working with my "orthodox" clients.

ANIME ABE

*Diversity is not a characteristic of life; it is a condition
necessary for life . . . like air and water.*
—Barry Lopez

It used to be said that most adolescents go through a period known as "storm and stress." Nowadays, that idea is not necessarily the case. Most individuals, regardless of their age, go through some very stormy and stressful periods in their lifetime. The teen years are years of adventure and a sense of invincibility for some, and awkwardness and isolation for others.

Abe was a socially awkward sixteen-year-old. His mother, who escorted him to the first session was dressed in very stylish clothing and seemed to have it all together. Oftentimes, it is difficult to hold back from making assumptions based on what you see in front of you, but my initial impressions are sometimes wrong. I met first with Abe's mother upon her request. I assured Abe that he would get his chance to talk with me, but he seemed busy reading an anime book. I took that to mean that he was indifferent over who got to talk first.

Abe's mother proved to be a poor historian of Abe's development, often confusing events with the wrong dates and, at times, the wrong child. By the time she finished her first ten minutes of nonstop talking, I was more confused than ever. She asked me whether she should get Abe. I told her that would be a good idea.

Abe walked into my room with his eyes still glued to the book. He plopped himself down on the couch, sitting more like a young child than a sixteen-year-old. I asked him, "What are you reading?"

"*Black Butler* by Yana Toboso," he responded in a monotone. I said, "Seems like a very interesting book. Do you mind if we put the book down and talk for a few minutes?" He reluctantly lowered the book from his face. I was immediately struck by the amount of makeup Abe had on. He wore eye shadow and lipstick, and his fingernails were painted as well. I asked him what the book was about, and he replied with a very detailed description. He asked, "Do you read anime?"

I said, "No, but I do enjoy reading other things."

"Like what?" he asked.

"I enjoy biographies, memoirs, and mostly nonfiction books." He countered with a "BORRRRING," stretching out the word for emphasis. I acknowledged that these books were probably not very interesting to many, and I told him that perhaps someday I would explore other genres of reading. (I had no intention of reading anime, although they do take up a huge amount of space at Barnes & Noble, so clearly many people enjoy it.)

I then went straight into the therapy process and asked him what brought him in today. He said, "My mother."

I asked, "Why did your mother bring you here?"

"She thinks I have no friends. I do have friends but most of them are virtual ones. I have a great relationship with most of them. We understand each other. I don't see it as a problem. Do you?"

"Well, are you happy with the friends you have?"

"Yes. They're cool," was his reply.

"So there must be something more that you or your mother haven't yet shared," I inquired, knowing that there was more hiding behind the makeup than just friendship issues.

"I want to have a sex change operation. She says no," Abe said, as if he was used to telling this to everyone he met.

Curious to get a better understanding of the family dynamics, I asked, "What does your dad have to say about the operation?"

"He doesn't know yet. We don't really talk much. He is a computer programmer, and we don't have much in common."

"Did your mother say why she did not want you to have the operation?" I pressed on.

"She said that she heard about others who did it and ended up committing suicide." He said this again as if he had had this discussion before.

"And you disagree with her research?" I asked.

"I don't know where she researched this, but I have been talking to others who are completely happy with their operation. I never wanted to be a boy. I feel trapped in a different body."

Now we were getting somewhere.

"At what age would you say you began to feel this way?" I asked, trying not to sound too much like a therapist.

"When I turned six, I used to play with dolls and dress up in my sister's clothes. Looking back, it felt so good, but I knew it would upset Mom and Dad so I didn't let them know what I was doing. But one day they caught me and screamed at me. Then they sent me to a shrink who told them that sometimes boys do that, so they laid off me for a while. When I got into fourth grade, I was only playing with other girls. I felt very good for a change. I no longer attempted to play sports with the guys. They all thought I was weird anyway."

We were getting to the end of the hour, so I had to find a way to end the session and also invite him back. I said, "Abe, your mom and dad are going to continue to have a difficult time with your situation. I suggest that you come back and talk some more next week. And please bring me an anime book so I can perhaps get a better understanding of what anime is." He gave me the thumbs up and agreed to come back the following week.

His mother, who was sitting in the waiting room, looked up and saw Abe smiling. Abe said, "See, even he wants to read anime." She shot me a look as if I was siding with Abe, and abruptly left.

Later in the week, I saw that Abe's mother had left a message on my machine. I called her back that night, and she said she was not sure this would work out. I sensed her hesitation and asked whether Abe told her he did not want to return. She said, "No, he does want to come talk to you. He is already looking for one of those silly books to give to you. I just don't want to have to pay you to try and identify with my son. He is a lost soul, and I need someone who can fix him."

"Fix him?" I asked incredulously.

"Yes. Get him to stop thinking about this operation. He is tearing the family apart. His father and I are separated, I don't see us getting back together, and adding this craziness will probably only isolate him from everyone else. I am also watching my mother dying in hospice and I cannot take this stress."

I responded, "I am sorry. I was unaware that your family was going through such experiences. I really feel that Abe will need someone to connect to as your family goes through these challenges, and I think he feels that he can trust me." She said she would think about it and get back to me. The next day she left a voicemail saying that she would bring Abe in for the Monday appointment.

Abe came into the session and seemed to be in a chipper mood. He handed me a book called *Vampire Knight*, from his anime collection. I asked him how he felt about our first session. He stated that he saw that I cared and was not judging him. This surprised him because he saw me as a religious man. He did not believe in God and disagreed with anyone who was a believer. He also made a request. He did not want me to refer to him as "he" or "him." I told him that I would try to honor his request but that I hoped he would forgive me and others if we slipped up from time to time. He said, "I heard your secretary say "He's here" when I came in but I didn't say anything." I commended him and reminded him that not everyone will be so understanding.

Abe sat down, this time seeming more focused on the conversation than on his books and fascination with anime. He announced that he was planning to attend the Otakon convention. I asked him to explain to me what that was because I was unfamiliar with the lingo. Abe explained that everyone dresses up, they show anime films and have panel discussions, and you can even learn to draw manga, among other things. Abe was very excited about the convention. He said his mother was making him pay for the majority of the ticket cost. Initially, he was upset that he should have to pay but eventually accepted the fact that his mother was not on board.

We spoke about his affinity that he developed for dressing in girls' clothing. Abe could not quite pinpoint what led him to cross-dressing. There was nothing traumatic in his childhood that precipitated his interest in it. He said it was just a yearning he had, one that at a young age he was not able to put into words. Now he could say that he had always felt that he had been put in the wrong body. He asked if I had ever felt that way.

At times in therapy you are asked personal questions. I was not expecting this question to be posed to me so early in a therapy relationship, but I had come to learn that Abe did not deal well with any answers that were not straightforward. He described both of his parents as sarcastic, and he did not like when they used sarcasm to try to humor him.

I went with the straightforward response. "I have never felt that way Abe, but I respect your feelings and would never judge you for how you feel. You are a caring and compassionate human being, and I see that you are very intelligent as well." He smiled and asked, "Is that a rare combination?" I explained that sometimes people who are very intelligent feel grossly misunderstood and thus become callous to the feelings of others. When I said that, Abe jumped up and exclaimed, "That's exactly how I feel! No one gets it, and no one gets me. I am not supported by my parents' feelings about my lifestyle; it really makes me feel lonely."

I attempted to shift gears with Abe and asked him to imagine that his parents were in the room and they just heard what he said. Then I asked Abe to close his eyes and picture the scene without saying a word. Abe complied with my directive. After he opened his eyes I could see that he was becoming tearful. In a weepy voice he said, "I guess they also might feel lonely and abandoned by me." I let the thought sit and waited for Abe to digest this and gather his wits.

I continued. "Abe, it is true that you are probably misunderstood, not just by your parents but by others who have nothing to do with the anime community. When you handed me this book and told me about the convention, I asked you to explain it so I could better understand what it was that you were interested in. How did you feel when I asked you for an explanation?"

"My initial thought was how could he not know about Otakon? But then I saw that you were genuinely interested in understanding anime. I appreciated that you were honest with me and that you wanted to get to know me better. Not many people do that."

"Abe, what if I read this book and told you next week that it was interesting but I prefer other reading material." I asked this question because I had once leafed through an anime book and didn't find the content particularly interesting.

Abe countered, "I would once again appreciate your honesty. Most people I know are not honest; they are hypocrites."

I asked for him to continue that thought about people being hypocritical. "I have had teachers who literally don't practice what they preach. My parents always told me to say *thank you* whenever someone gave me something as a gift. I never saw them saying *thank you* to people at stores. They say, "Gimmee two dozen donuts and a cup of coffee." I will always say *thank you* because I know it is the right thing to do."

"Thank you," I said, and we both laughed.

Using his last thought about thankfulness I decided to prod on. "Abe, others will continue to not understand you. They might make rude comments to you or look at you in a funny way. I cannot say you will have an easy time going forward, but I will be here to support you as a person. Your family is your family. Thanking them even though you might feel they are hypocritical or lacking understanding of what you are going through will only serve to benefit you in the future. As you mentioned before, they are having a hard time with your transition and will need support. They will also get funny looks when they are with you at times. I will try to support your parents too, but you are my top priority. But remember, they will make mistakes, as we all do." Abe smiled and thanked me.

We continued our sessions for a few months. Abe and his parents seemed to understand each other better. Abe proved to be a very insightful person and understood how his black and white thinking style was not always conducive to dealing with others who are uncultured in the anime lifestyle.

Our sessions progressed well. My understanding of the culture was as good as it was going to get. I was also going through a slight transition as I was thinking of pursuing more of a teaching career. I explained to Abe that I might be leaving the clinic but would continue to work with him privately if he would like me to. Abe felt that he had reached a level of understanding. Abe thanked me, as did his parents. I do not know what became of Abe. Who knows? Perhaps Abe is now a popular manga artist.

Reflecting back on Abe, I was struck by a couple of questions and assumptions that Abe posed over the course of our sessions. One was the question of whether I ever felt I was in the wrong body. The other was the assumption that religious therapists could not provide quality therapy to an atheist client. I talked to other religious therapists to get a better understanding, but most of them stated that they had never had a client who was an atheist. Religious people tend to seek out religious therapists. Nowadays, with the advent of Google, many clients do a fair amount of research about a therapist before deciding to work with them.

As Abe was an atheist, it was unclear whether or not the social issues stemmed from the general population not having a great understanding of transgender individuals or whether there was some incompatibility between Abe's thought process and religion or authority in general.

I believe that religious therapists can treat atheists, gay therapists can treat straight people, black therapists can treat white people, and so on. Most people would specifically choose someone who resembles them in most ways. I do believe that the most competent therapists are the ones who are constantly keeping up to date with various cultures and their specific needs. Understanding which modality works best is very helpful.

To increase my own cultural sensitivity, I began reading books on multicultural psychology. I highly recommend Derald Sue's articles on becoming a culturally competent therapist. I have taught courses in Multicultural Psychology at Notre Dame of Maryland and at Stevenson University, and I believe that I got more out of those classes than any others that I have taught— or taken.

Working with Abe also made me wonder how many more people feel they were born in the wrong body and how grossly misunderstood and alienated they must feel. This is an intriguing question. I would have to give that more thought.

THE LONELY GENIUS

As you become more clear about who you really are, you'll be better able to decide what is best for you the first time around.
—Oprah Winfrey

I am often motivated and stimulated by intelligent clients. Every therapist has clients that they truly look forward to working with and those with whom they are anxiously waiting for the hour to end. If they tell you otherwise they are lying. I have never heard any honest therapist say that they enjoy working with all clients equally. Certain personalities grate on our nerves, and it is best to talk to a supervisor or a colleague when this happens. Notice I said *when* and not *if*.

Intelligent people tend to suffer in silence. They suffer from a sense of loneliness that often comes from being grossly misunderstood. I grew up with many very smart people, and I really liked them although I never felt I was a match for them, intellectually. I made a common error and attributed my self-disparaging attitude to my sub-par grades. I never invested much time in studying while in school, and I later regretted that. I wasn't a great test-taker especially when it came to multiple-choice questions. I preferred playing sports, listening to music, and reading mysteries over studying.

I remember going home in a carpool one Friday afternoon. The carpool consisted of four very smart boys (who were all part of the non-existent Mensa club at our small school) and me. One day the woman driving the car asked each one of us our scores on a big test that we had all just taken. "101," replied Eli. "103," replied Danny. "104," from Sam. "100," from Dave. "And Jonathan, what did you get?"

"I got a 63, but my teacher said I am doing much better." Although I felt like an idiot, I tried not to care too much. I was just looking forward to playing football later that day.

It was not until my junior year in high school when things started to click for me. I worked a bit harder and became more interested in the future. My fully formed frontal lobes were finally prepared for the abstract reasoning that would help improve my scholarship. I continued to carpool with Eli, Danny, Dave, and Sam, but the carpool driver never again asked about our grades.

My interest in psychology continued to be stimulated. This was partially due to the quiet influence of my father and my knack for learning how to attend to people's troubles without shying away from crises. Throughout college and graduate school, I continued to evolve as a serious thinker who could still have a good time on the side. I took up the saxophone and would sing at parties and weddings. However, the daytime hours were mostly spent being stimulated by a brilliant rabbi who demonstrated that psychology is everywhere. I continued my studies in religious education and Talmudic law and developed a very good balance of philosophical reasoning and clinical ability. I decided that a career in psychology would be the logical choice, after toying only briefly with the idea of going to medical school. My reasoning was rather simple. Physicians have a general prescription for most physical ailments. Someone with strep is treated with antibiotics. Pain is treated with analgesics. Where is the challenge in medicine?

However, in psychology, no two human conditions can possibly be treated exactly the same. So I began graduate school and loved almost every minute of it.

After graduate school, I began seeing clients and continued being fascinated by the brilliant minds that mentored me, as well as the brilliant ones who eventually became clients of mine. Bill was one such client.

Bill came to me with a presenting problem of chronic pain. A presenting problem, for those readers who are non-clinicians, is not necessarily the underlying problem. Bill had chronic pain in his lower back, his buttocks, and his feet. After taking a detailed history, which Bill eloquently and thoroughly described, we proceeded with hypnotherapy techniques, which are often the most effective prescribed treatment for patients who suffer from chronic pain. I have seen tremendous success with my clients who use hypnotherapy to help them alleviate their pain symptoms and would advocate its use over pain medication for most clients.

Bill was in his mid-seventies. He was a heavyset engineer who outshined all of his peers with his intellect. He could

outdo most university professors in terms of articulating difficult concepts into chunks of palatable information. He had a
Ph.D. and two master's degrees, which he admitted were just
for the fun of it. He was also a master storyteller. He was married to an English professor named Martha who taught at a
nearby college in the suburbs of Boston. They had a cordial
relationship with one another and got along well on an intellectual level but were seriously deprived in terms of intimacy
and emotional connectivity. When questioned about how he
felt about their lack of intimacy, Bill stated that he was not so
concerned. I wondered whether that was the truth.

Bill possessed an IQ that would probably be said to be "off
the charts." Some people would be envious of such high IQ. I
am not one of these people. In fact, I feel for them. They are
grossly misunderstood, and they often do not like therapy or
therapists because they choose logic over emotion. There indeed seems to be a significant correlation between those with
a high IQ and those with a low EQ, or emotional intelligence.
There is distance between the head and the heart.

Bill would often share philosophical quotes and stories of
how he was able to understand things that most humans could
not. He made the common mistake that most geniuses make:
he expected everyone whom he interacted with to be just as
smart as he was. This explains why people like Bill have zero
patience in grocery store lines or at stoplights—stupid clerks
and stupid drivers. So they end up in professions where they
can show off their true superior capabilities and sometimes in
classrooms teaching bright, vulnerable college students (who

might actually believe that their professor invented string theory).

People like Bill tend to be socially withdrawn. Bill was slightly different because he had a very well-developed sense of humor. The combination of humor and intellect enabled him to develop some significant friendships. His humor and intellect also invigorated me as a therapist. I was excited for my sessions with Bill. Bill responded very well to hypnotherapy. At times he would be "lights out" before I'd even said anything. He was programmed to fall into trance states like a Pavlovian dog.

After the sixth session, Bill related an entirely different issue that had been bothering him. He was troubled by his homosexual fantasies. He had never acted on them, but he could not ignore their existence. Despite his relationship with his wife and a few friends, he felt left out and misunderstood. He was indeed gifted—gifted, but troubled, and extremely lonely.

Bill related during that sixth session that he felt like people would look at him differently if they knew the truth about him. And he firmly believed that he was the only person in the world who had homosexual thoughts that plagued him on a daily basis.

As I mentioned earlier, the presenting problem is not necessarily the underlying problem for most clients. At the same time that Bill revealed his secret fantasies, his pain symptoms had nearly disappeared. It could be attributed to the hypnotherapy, his motivation, or the revelation of his homosexual fantasies, fantasies that he had never before shared with anyone.

The rest of our sessions dealt with Bill's fantasy life, which disturbed him greatly. If Sigmund Freud had met Bill, he would say that Bill was employing the defense mechanism of intellectualization. And Freud would not be wrong. Bill would share his secrets with very little emotion. He tried to conceptualize his desire to become sexual with another man using eloquent prose, quoting from Greek mythology and finding validity for his thoughts and feelings through the works of Nietzsche and Socrates. I always enjoy a deep philosophical discussion, and my talks with Bill were indeed always fascinating. But I still felt bad for Bill. At that time, Bill lacked the capacity to move from his head to his heart.

At one point Bill looked at me and asked how I felt he was doing in therapy. This is always a difficult question to answer instinctively and is never a good question to answer impulsively. So I did what I was trained to do.

"Why are you asking me this question at this point of our therapeutic relationship?" After a long pregnant pause, Bill revealed what I thought was on his mind.

"Doc, I am very embarrassed about this." (Therapeutic silence. Shifting in his seat. Here it comes.)

"Doc, after my sessions with you, I seem to have stronger homosexual urges. Again, I would never act on them, and I can't even believe I am sharing this with you. But after we end our sessions I feel intellectually stimulated, which also arouses me in other ways. Sometimes my thoughts are about you, and other times they are about other people with whom I have had wonderfully intellectually stimulating encounters."

Now, it is common for clients to enter into the Freudian world of transference where they begin to project feelings, whether positive or negative, onto their therapist. I remained with my typical poker face and let him continue to explore.

"This does not make logical sense to me. I trust you and know that what we discuss here is confidential, but why would my conversations with you and other intelligent people lead me to sexual fantasies?" he wondered aloud.

I explained to Bill that stimulation is stimulation no matter what. "When your brain is stimulated, other parts of your body can also become stimulated. When you achieve insight because of something a therapist—or anyone for that matter— says, you become attracted to the person you are having that conversation with. It's only natural."

Long pause. More shifting.

"Are you saying that I am only capable of feeling on a physical, sexual, or emotional level when stimulated intellectually?"

"Bill, remember you told me that after you have an intellectual conversation, you feel pain-free until you get home? When you are intellectually stimulated, you are releasing endorphins that make you feel good, and your pain is eliminated."

Bill was having an "Aha!" moment, and it was very evident. Bill slowly got up, shook my hand and thanked me. The next session Bill came in with a big smile.

"I think I have some peace of mind now. My physical pain is gone, and I am starting to understand the emotional brain. I don't think I will give up on studying philosophy, but I will become a better listener. "By the way," Bill said with a wink of his eye, "I think you really enjoyed our sessions together as much as I did." I just smiled back, certain that the only counter-transference I was having with Bill was a little envy at his ability to tell an amazing tale.

Bill continued therapy with me for about four more months. Over this time period, Bill felt significant relief from his pain. We had stopped using hypnotherapy and ventured more into the existential realm of therapy.

During another session, Bill said to me, out of the blue, "You know, death does not scare me."

"Why are you saying that, and what made you bring this up now?" I asked.

"Well last week, after my session with you, I spoke with my attorney about revising my will. I have been thinking of various charities where I would like to gift a great portion of my money. Of course, my alma mater would receive a significant amount. I would like to have a scholarship fund in my family name. I know this would bring joy to my wife, should I pre-decease her, which I plan to do." He looked up at me for a second, trying to register my reaction as he said this. "I would also like to donate my brain and other organs to science. Hopefully they will gain much from my brain," he said with a wink and a smile. "Anyway, I was thinking about my impending demise, and I look forward to seeing for myself whether or not there is an afterlife. And if there is one, I would be excited to be an active participant of whatever that entails."

I was shocked at Bill's words. "Bill, you have just said a lot, and I am somewhat perplexed. Perhaps we will need more time to digest all of this. However, I must first ask, are you terminally ill and if you are, why are you first telling me this huge piece of news now?"

Without missing a beat, Bill said, "I thought you would ask that. The answer is yes; I have terminal cancer and I refuse to go for chemotherapy. I want my brain to be donated to science without all the pollutants. I never shared this with you because I did not want you to treat me as a terminally ill man."

I honestly would never have known Bill was terminally ill. I admired his courage to approach his illness with such fortitude and, dare I say, delight. He seemed stronger than ever and had not missed a beat in terms of his intellectual pursuit of life's deeper meaning.

Bill continued. "I was reading *Man's Search for Meaning* by Victor Frankl and was very impressed with his work. I had never heard of logotherapy before, and I wanted to discuss this existential dilemma with you and why I don't seem to be in crisis. I think I have already found meaning in my existence. I think my wife will also be okay with my death. She knows that I will not be around much longer. She is a very practical woman and has already made many of the arrangements.

The doctors say I don't have much time, and I figured it would only be fair to prepare you at this point."

After thanking Bill for his consideration in letting me know that our sessions together were reaching their endpoint I said, "Well, you seem to have it figured out, Bill. So what did you want to discuss with me about the meaning of life?"

"As a religious man, I was interested in your take on suffering and death."

We had a nice philosophical discussion about logotherapy and meaning, in general. Bill seemed pleased with my responses and was very explorative and intuitive. It was evident that he had studied religion during his lifetime, and he was as good of a student as he was a teacher.

Two months later, my supervisor informed me that Bill had passed away. Although I did not show my emotions to my supervisor, in my car I paused to shed a few tears for Bill.

I spent much of the next two weeks thinking of Bill. I knew I would really miss our sessions together. I had learned so much from him, as he claimed to have learned from me. I was happy that I was able to ease his physical pain and some of the emotional pain he was suffering from. I still miss Bill to this day. Even writing this story brings back a flood of memories of the extraordinary moments we spent together. I am curious to know which institution was the lucky recipient of his magnificent brain.

Streaming and Dreaming

What makes you vulnerable makes you beautiful.
—Brené Brown

One of the joys in working as a mental health professional is encountering a client whom you have not seen for a while, someone who seemed to have fared well because of (or despite!) your therapeutic intervention. One day, I received an intriguing letter in the mail with an unfamiliar address. Even though I was curious, I set it down with my other mail and went inside for dinner. After all, family time is family time.

Once the kids were taken care of, I took the heap of mail to my office. Nowadays, mail is quick and easy to go through—mostly junk ads and offers for new credit cards. Anything that says "0% interest" on the front goes straight into the recycle bin. How many credit cards could one possibly want or need?

The letter had a return address in Florida. It turned out to be a card from someone named Julie. I had no idea who this was, but then I read the personal message.

Dear Dr. Lasson,

I am here today because I needed someone to believe in me. I cannot think of anyone else in my life that influenced me as much as you did. When I was in fifth grade you saw me for a few sessions after my father passed away. I was having a miserable time and had practically given up, socially and academically. You kept telling me that I had so much potential. I had heard that before from other therapists but it never came as genuinely as it came from you. You also repeatedly told me that you wanted an invitation to my graduation. Well here it is. I have finished high school and was accepted into the college that was first on my list. All because you taught me to believe in myself. I would be honored if you would attend my graduation but please do not feel obligated. I know you are busy, but just know that I am thinking of you and I thank you for bringing me to this place.

Yours truly,
Julie

I was touched by Julie's kind sentiment and thoughtfulness. I slowly began to remember Julie, a fifth-grader who had just gone through a terrible loss. Her father had been diagnosed with pancreatic cancer and passed quickly. I went to my files and looked through Julie's folder, which was relatively thin as I had only seen her for a short period of time. Despite my messy, brief handwritten notes, I was able to get the gist of our sessions together. Slowly I pieced together the sessions held years before. I have noticed that oftentimes when my notes are brief, it is because I am paying extra attention to the client's body language or the therapeutic approach involves either play or art. This was certainly true in Julie's case.

Julie had drawn pictures, which is something that I have always felt helped children with emotional expression. She was not the most artistic fifth-grader, but she did express herself quite well through her art. Originally her pictures were in black and white. Toward the end of our sessions together, they became more colorful and alive. This is common with children for whom therapy ends up having a meaningful impact. Color in pictures is indicative of being more in tune with your emotions. She worked hard on these pictures and would often spend time admiring them and asking me for my approval. We explored the meaning of her pictures together, and she proved to be very insightful for a ten-year-old.

Memories of our sessions together came flooding back to me. When Julie first came to see me, her mother remained in the waiting room, anxious for the part of the session where I talk with the parent. Julie presented as a rather small, young girl with a very thin frame. She carried with her a journal and a stuffed toy dog that she would bring out from time to time during our sessions.

I brought out my feelings chart and asked Julie to point to the feelings she had when she first heard about her father's illness and after she found out that he passed away. She told me that at first it was hard to cry. She had been more concerned with her mother than her own emotions. We talked about her fears and the things she loved. We talked about school and friends. Julie would usually give very short responses and would ask to draw instead. After our fourth session, I saw that Julie was beginning to evolve.

Julie, who initially had been very reserved, began to open up and shared with me her deepest feelings and fears. She was very scared of illness as she saw her father being eaten away by bad cells. She hated hospitals and anything medical. She talked about herself dying and how unfair it was that God took her father away. She lamented how he would not be there at her birthdays, her graduation, or her wedding. Many of her original drawings were of hospital beds containing people hooked up to IVs and bodies ravaged by illness, as indicated in her drawings with huge, ugly black dots. The sadness on her face after handing me the drawings each week told her life story since her father's illness and subsequent death. After a few sessions though, it seemed Julie was done talking about death and wanted to move on.

The rapport between Julie and me was improving and she began to look forward to our sessions. We talked about what she liked most about the time she had spent with her father. At first she would try to draw pictures of those times, but eventually she would put down the colored pencils and just talk to me. She told me about the times she would go stream-hiking with her dad. She loved nature and adored animals. She was fearless of nature but quite fearful of reality. Nature allowed her to dream. Her mother did not share the same interests as her father, and Julie could not convince her mother to go stream-hiking with her. Her mother did allow her to join the Girl Scouts. She brought me Girl Scout cookies from time to time and would talk easily about her different adventures. I was quite surprised that this skinny, young girl who initially was so reserved had become so talkative and intuitive.

I thought back to what had been the turning point for Julie. I pulled out a picture that she had drawn of a stream and recalled a dream that she had told me. In the dream she was walking hand in hand with her father down a beautiful stream. Even though the stream was very rocky, they were able to navigate the rocks because they were experts. In the dream she was laughing at her father's funny stories when her father slipped and fell down a steep incline. She looked down and could not find him. There was no one around when she called out his name. She ran away, and then woke up in a cold sweat.

I usually do not process dreams with young children as they are not at a level to glean much from interpretation. However, Julie was exceptional so I asked her what she thought of her dream. She said that it was hard to tell. The man she was holding hands with was definitely her father, but his face had no resemblance to that of her father's. She asked me if that made sense. I told her that happens a lot with dreams.

She said, "I think the dream was also about a man I wish I knew better. I felt so guilty that I was not able to find him after he fell."

I ventured one interpretation: "Streams sometimes represent living life to its fullest. When the stream is flowing we are living. At times the stream hits a rock, and it slows the stream down. Eventually, the stream will continue."

Julie thought about this for a while and said, "Dr. Lasson, I think things will work out but there will be bumps in the road. Just like the stream, it will keep on flowing. Even if it dries up at times, it will eventually get refilled."

I was amazed at Julie's thoughtful response. I had nothing more to add. Not only was Julie able to process her feelings, but she added her own insight.

When children are confronted with the humbling reality of death, they usually close up and have a difficult time processing their emotions. Julie was a special child with a very special father.

When I met Julie's mother, she confided that she was envious of the relationship that Julie had with her father. She remarked how special a man her father was. He never missed any of Julie's parent-teacher conferences, school plays, or karate classes.

Julie's mom continued to meet with me for the last few minutes of each session. Julie was very concerned about her mom and how lonely and sad she seemed. I told her mom how concerned Julie was about her and referred her to a support group. She attended and seemed to be doing better. Julie had made significant progress and went off to camp that summer with a newfound sense of confidence. She met two other children at camp who had also lost a parent, and they became good friends.

Julie still loved nature and would often go down to the stream, realizing that sometimes streams dry up but they eventually get refilled. She used this analogy to sustain her motivation. Julie indeed kept on going. Even when there were bumps in the road, Julie continued on her mission.

I was not able to attend Julie's graduation but I called her, and we spoke for a while. I asked her what she planned to do after she graduated. She said, "I want become a therapist, just like you!" How could I not cry? With tears of joy streaming down my cheeks, I thought of the valuable lesson this young girl had taught herself—and me—about life.

NO MUSIC THERAPY ALLOWED!

I was born with music inside me. It was a force already within me when I arrived on the scene. It was a necessity for me-like food and water. —Ray Charles

I began my internship at Baywood Island Psychiatric Hospital in December of 1998. Located in South Florida, Baywood served two major psychiatric populations: geriatric patients and those with dual diagnoses. Dual diagnoses, at least back in those days, referred to individuals with a psychiatric condition along with an addiction.

At the time, a wonderful woman with a very colorful personality ran the internship program. There were eight interns (seven women and I), and much of our work was spent doing monotonous write-ups on these sessions. The notes all started to look the same after a while as many of the sessions started and ended the same way. "Not too much progress"...or "very little progress noted." Achieving any significant improvement with geriatric patients suffering from chronic mental illness is very difficult. Getting them to talk is almost equivalent to saving their lives.

Many of the geriatric patients were elderly Jewish residents of Broward County whose children felt it would be a good idea to have them spend their time in a day program. Some of the children fondly referred to their elderly parents as *alte cockers,* Yiddish that translates more or less to *old farts* in English. Although this may sound derogatory, it's a common term that even the patients use to describe themselves.

We interns were primarily charged with providing these elderly patients process-oriented therapy. How you conduct process-oriented therapy with eighty-year-olds suffering from dementia still remains an elusive mystery to me. Process therapy tends to emphasize movement and body feeling, a holistic approach to help patients with psychiatric illnesses become better attuned to what their bodies are telling them. But my group rarely moved at all!

Looking back, those sessions reminded me of the fantastic movie starring Robert De Niro and Robin Williams, *Awakenings.* Imagine the scene. Nurses are wheeling patients into a room where a therapist is conducting a session. No one is moving a muscle, let alone talking. They were essentially catatonic. The movie could have been filmed at Baywood Island Psychiatric Hospital. It seemed that any type of intervention with this population would be an exercise in futility. I felt hopeless.

After a couple of weeks of processing with the geriatric patients, I asked one of my fellow interns, "Is this what we signed up for?" She just put their hands up and said we should be happy we got an internship. Several people from our co-hort hadn't been matched with an internship at all and had to wait another year to apply! I guess we had to look at the positive side of things.

Aside from the occasional calls to subdue a combative patient in the other unit, the job was pretty dull—except on one occasion. For some reason, the hospital accidentally placed two patients who both believed they were Jesus in the same room in the inpatient ward. This led to some great theological—and physical—battles until at last the two Jesuses were separated into different rooms.

I decided it was time to think creatively. I wanted to use my time wisely and try to make some difference in the lives of my patients. I was always taught that if you can make some-one happy, even for a moment, then you have improved the quality of their lives. I learned this lesson from watching the real-life Patch Adams (the movie starring Robin Williams was based on his life) as he was doing rounds at Coastal Hospital in Miami Beach. Dressed in his clown suit, he entertained the oncology ward with his antics. Seeing him enhance the quality of life for these cancer patients was a wonderful experience, and Patch Adams became one of my all-time heroes.

I wanted to do something, something more than routine process therapy. I've always had a love for music—and I even have some talent to go with it—so during a session I began humming an old Yiddish tune. I looked around and to my astonishment I saw two essentially catatonic patients begin to nod their heads and tap on rhythm. This was amazing! I continued singing with them for two weeks and saw the quality of their lives improve ever so slightly. Until one day when the coordinator came by and peered into my room. After my session, this well-intentioned woman called me into her office. "What do you think you are doing?" she wanted to know.

"I am processing with my patients," I innocently responded. "That's not processing! You are singing with them."

I replied with a sense of confidence, "True, but we are processing what we are singing." She insisted that I was not supposed to be doing music therapy. I agreed; I am not a music therapist, after all. However, I argued that the patients' quality of life was improving. They began to smile more and even experience lapses of lucidity. She gave me a look that said "whatever" and left me alone. My intuition told me that my out-of-the-box approach of using music to improve the quality of the lives of geriatric patients was right on track. Having watched my own elderly relatives, I knew that music is one thing that remains embedded in memories even after most cognitive functions have ceased. I still remember my grandmother singing familiar tunes in the latter stages of Alzheimer's. Music goes deep. I continued to rock with the *alte cockers*.

Religious Guilt

Guilt is to our spirit, what pain is to our body! —David Bednar

Many of my private clients happen to be religious. Some specifically chose me because they googled me, found out that I was also religious, and wanted a therapist who could understand their cultural needs. Others had been former students of mine who found me to be a non-judgmental person whom they could talk to about religious guilt.

Rivka came to me at the suggestion of a friend of hers who was a former student of mine. She came into the office somewhat anxious as this was her first experience in therapy. She stood waiting for direction until I pointed her to an easy chair. After going through the preliminary forms I immediately addressed the anxiety issue: "You seem very anxious." (I am very observant. They actually teach psychology students to pick up on these things!) Rivka admitted that she had not been able to sleep for the past week since she made the initial appointment with me over the phone. I validated her concerns. (They teach us that too.)

Rivka was a twenty-one-year-old student attending a religious college for girls. She wanted to become a speech pathologist and earn enough to support the future husband who she imagined would be in rabbinical school. Rivka was the second of four children and seemed to be of average to high-average intellect. Her presenting problem was that she had test-taking anxiety. Every time she would take a test she would freeze up and forget most of what she had studied. Despite her test anxiety she managed to hold her own, maintaining a 3.5 GPA throughout college.

As mentioned, therapists must look beyond the presenting problem in order to become successful. Getting a more detailed history from Rivka was slightly more difficult than usual as she was reluctant to share things about her past. My hunch was that she had not always been religious but became religious in her late teens. My hunch proved to be correct.

Rivka had attended public school until ninth grade. She then went on a trip to Israel in the summer before tenth grade. She had been very inspired by that trip and wanted to learn more about her relatives and her heritage. It turns out that her great-grandparents were religious Jews who perished in Nazi Germany. Deeply moved by this revelation, she begged her parents to allow her to visit Auschwitz where her great-grandparents had been killed. Although not religious, her parents arranged for her to go on a trip with other local teens, called the *March of the Living*. The March of the Living takes unaffiliated Jewish teens to visit the site of the concentration camps and then Israel, which was a common path for many Holocaust survivors.

Going to Auschwitz and then to Israel changed Rivka's life. She was now on a mission. She wanted to know more about what she referred to as "authentic" Judaism. She told me that her parents did not follow the ways of her great-grandparents, and she demanded to know why. Her parents attempted to explain that the family was bitter at God for allowing such a tragedy to occur, so they had abandoned the Jewish way of life, for the most part.

Rivka had not always gone by the name Rivka. Until she was a sophomore in high school, she went by her name given at birth, Rebecca. Most of her friends and family called her Becky. It was only after attending Hebrew school that she insisted on Rivka, the Hebrew version of her given name. After eleventh grade, Rivka convinced her parents to send her to a religious school.

Reluctant at first, Rivka's parents conceded when her grandfather said that he knew the principal, and that he would pay for it. Rivka never looked back. Although she was far behind her peers in her knowledge of Hebrew and Judaic studies in general, she learned quickly and caught up. After high school she visited Israel again, spending a year there and feeling on top of the world.

When Rivka returned home, she enrolled in a girl's seminary and began her undergraduate studies. She kept up with her Judaic studies as well. She said that at around nineteen years old her anxiety began to take hold. She recalled sitting in class when it happened. She was taking a test and seemingly out of nowhere she began to hyperventilate. She immediately got up and ran out of the classroom, feeling lightheaded and nauseous. Her teacher ran out to see what was wrong and found her curled up in a fetal position on the bathroom floor. She was sent to the hospital, but the doctors could not find anything medically wrong with her. They suggested that perhaps Rivka had experienced a panic attack.

Just retelling this story caused Rivka anxiety. I suggested that we switch topics and talk more about her family. She talked about her brother and two sisters. Rivka was quick to point out that they were not religious. I questioned her as to why that was the first thing she wanted me to know about her siblings. Sensing that perhaps there was a reason for this, I surmised that she was not very close with her family anymore and conjectured that maybe she was ashamed of them. I assured her that she was not being judged and that she could feel free to explore more openly. She stated that her brother had a girlfriend, who Rivka did not like. She could not pinpoint what she did not like about her. I suggested that maybe she was upset that he had a girlfriend, period. She acknowledged that this was true as well. Our time was almost up. "Think about what we discussed today, and we'll continue next time from where we left off," I said. She scheduled another session for later that week.

When dealing with clients, especially religious people, I always work on the supposition that guilt might be the driving force behind most of their psychological problems. When Rivka came for the second session, she still seemed somewhat anxious, although a bit more relaxed. We processed why this was so. She stated that I seemed to be nonjudgmental. She also displayed a little bit of humor this time and said that she always had a "certain perception" of therapists. She stated that for a therapist, I seemed pretty normal. I took it as a compliment. I informed her once again that what we discuss is confidential, and we continued.

"I thought a lot about what we talked about last session, and I realized that I am at fault for what has happened to my family." Seeing my confused look, she continued, "not the ones who died in the Holocaust, but my bad relationship with my siblings." She went on to say that she would like to make amends with her siblings for imposing her newfound religious beliefs on them and needed some guidance as to how to do that.

"Rivka," I said to her, "before you make amends with your siblings, I think you really need to make amends with yourself." She wanted some clarification. "You see Rivka, before you became religious you led a life similar to that of your siblings. You never thought much about that?" Rivka nodded. Conjecturing, I asked, "Did you have a boyfriend?" (Get the tissues ready, Doc.)

Rivka, with tears welling up, revealed that she had had several boyfriends and that she had done some things in the past that she now regretted. As a result, she had become somewhat obsessive about some of her religious rituals. I noticed that her hands were chapped almost to the point of being bloody. "Like hand-washing?"

She smiled and looked at her hands. "You are observant!" We both smiled.

We then discussed how her hand-washing obsession might be an over-compensation for feeling like she had defiled herself with her past actions. She admitted that was true and began to cry. When she stopped crying, she asked what she should do, because her anxiety was becoming more pronounced. We talked about her learning to forgive herself, and I referred her to a female colleague of mine who could help her deal with some of the issues she had concerning guilt.

Once she released herself from the shackles of guilt, her test anxiety began to diminish. She was also ready to approach her siblings and ask for forgiveness.

Many people, especially those who become more religious later in life, feel ashamed of their past. The goal of the therapist is to empower the client to learn from the past and accept themselves for who they were and appreciate who they have become. An important facet of therapy is to teach clients how to continue a relationship with those who have not chosen the same path that they have. Rivka had been inspired by her trip to Poland and Israel and was upset when her family didn't share her enthusiasm.

Part of my therapy with Rivka was to help her learn how to see in ways other than black or white and all or nothing. I demonstrated this idea with the Hermanic Grid, a sort of optical illusion where you look at a black and white grid and begin to see gray circles. When Rivka stared at the black squares and saw shades of gray, she understood: not all Jews practice Judaism the same way.

Life transitions—spiritual epiphanies—are very personal. Those going through such transitions sometimes have the unrealistic expectation that others should keep the same pace. Eventually Rivka was able to see that imposing her newfound personal beliefs on her family was unfair. She understood that it was possible to live harmoniously with her relatives, even though they were not particularly religious.

Much of my therapy with religious people is helping them accept their past and inoculate them from the unhealthy and counter-productive forms of guilt that are the most prominent precursors of mental illness. Rivka continued seeing the therapist to whom I referred her. She began to make progress and accept her family—and herself—for who they were.

AFTERWORD

My journey from
"guilt ridden" to "guilt riddance"

At a social event, an acquaintance of mine came up to me and suggested that I form a "psychological" travel agency. I asked him what that meant. He said, "You can take people on ego trips and guilt trips." Not a bad idea. Not in my future plans either. However, his suggestion ignited the switch that made the wheels in my brain turn. I thought about guilt trips. And I thought some more. I came to the realization that most of my clients suffer from some form of guilt of varying degrees of severity. Some become depressed, others become anxious, and still others become obsessed with the issue that is causing these guilt feelings.

In a few of the tales contained within this book, I attempted to show the reader how these feelings usually come out after the initial presenting problem has been discussed. It is actually the underlying guilt that is paralyzing the client from making significant progress in overcoming their problems, whether they are related to depression, anxiety, relationships, or whatever.

It's important to consider that much of our self-imposed guilt comes from the "If only I could have" feeling. Consider the following example of Robert, a paramedic who had worked as a volunteer for over ten years. On one particular call, Robert remembers how difficult a time he had navigating the snowy streets because he had forgotten to put chains on his tires. He had also forgotten to put back the chainsaw he usually kept in his pickup truck in case of emergency. On the way to the call he came across a tree that had fallen across the street, blocking any entry into the neighborhood. By the time Robert was able to find an alternative route, it was too late. The sixty-four-year-old man he was supposed to help had passed away.

Robert's initial feeling was of intense guilt. He blamed the man's death on his forgetting to put chains on his tires and the chainsaw in his truck. In reality, even if he did have the proper equipment, who says he would have been able to save the man? What Robert failed to recognize, due to his intense guilt feelings, was that there are some things that are simply beyond our control.

Lawrence Kohlberg, a pioneer in understanding the moral development in children, discusses in great length the subject of how and when children develop a sense of conscience based on basic morals. He differentiates between pre-conventional, conventional, and post-conventional forms of moral development. Much has been discussed and written since Kohlberg came up with his theories. However, one thing remains constant. Guilt is prevalent in all ages and in all cultures.

Some suggest that guilt is more prevalent among religious people, while others would suggest the opposite. Since religiously minded people have a mechanism to absolve themselves of guilt feelings, they might fare better. Others might argue that religion magnifies the guilt.

Looking back at my early years, even *Sesame Street* left me wondering what is right and wrong. I kind of related to Bert, who was always more concerned about others than Ernie, who seemed oblivious. I thought Ernie should feel bad about all the pain and worry he caused Bert.

I had a roommate in my early college years, Abe, who was an obsessive-compulsive. He insisted his alarm clock be situated at a precise 45-degree angle to his bed and that his hairbrush be perpendicular to the alarm clock. He would carefully pluck all the hairs out of his brush each night, and he would measure with a ruler exactly how much deodorant he had left in the deodorant stick. Some guys decided to have fun with Abe. They turned his alarm clock upside down, filled his brush with all sorts of different colored hairs, and replaced the deodorant in the stick with frozen peaches. As you can imagine, Abe went crazy. I felt bad for Abe but was powerless against these guys.

The guilt of seeing others suffer and not doing anything about it is perhaps what propelled my interest in the mental health field. I checked out library books and read up on obsessive-compulsive disorder, anxiety disorders, and depression. I was very sensitive to these individuals who were so misunderstood, and I felt upset with those who made their mental illness worse by teasing them about it. I know they were not intentionally mean people, but it's easy to get sucked up in a vacuum of meanness when others around you are acting in such a way.

Guilt over watching people suffer and not doing anything about it is common. It sometimes causes people to do something constructive and finally take some action to combat their apathy. They might start helping people suffering from illness. Others, on the other hand, might resort to wallowing in depression over their inaction.

In order for a therapist—or anyone—to deal with someone else's guilt issues, they have to be in recovery, recovery from unresolved issues that stem from their own guilt. I have realized over my years as a therapist that I am ineffective in dealing with some types of issues and will refer potential clients to other practitioners if I feel the client's problem is hitting too close to home. That, I believe, is the responsible thing to do. Other colleagues would say one should work through their guilt issues. I respectfully disagree with that standpoint and have chosen my own modus operandi. The journey from "guilt ridden" to "guilt riddance" can be a long one for some, and it would be unfair to subject my clients to ineffective therapy.

The fact is that everyone makes mistakes. Therapists are no exception to the rule. We say or do the right things—or we do not say or do the right things—in therapy. I have been "guilty" of both. How we deal with our guilt is crucial. If we perseverate, as I tend to do, we will not be able to function effectively as therapists.

At this stage of my career, I no longer dwell on issues of guilt that I have already adequately processed. I need to move on, just as I tell the clients with whom I work. If some are upset with me, so be it. I consult with colleagues on a regular basis. Sometimes they put me in my place; sometimes I feel validated for my behavior.

What has empowered me to move beyond guilt? The answer is my age. This revelation came to me when discussing with a relative a situation that was going on in an organization she had run successfully for many years. She was being bullied and harassed by the parent of one of the children she worked with and said to herself, "I am forty years old and do not deserve to be treated this way." As Albert Einstein put it, "I have reached an age when, if someone tells me to wear socks, I don't have to."

What is it about age that helps us feel less guilty? Is it just that we are getting older and more forgetful? We tend to forget the things that people say to us that are hurtful and insulting and we move on. In truth, age provides us some degree of respect for our years of experience. Those who have matured to the extent that we realize we cannot dwell on the past are in good shape. Age has certainly enabled me to take stock of my life and realize that I can assert myself better if I leave the guilt behind.

I remember a particular class I attended. The instructor continually put down the students for what he perceived as not caring about what he had to offer. The individuals in this class were, for the most part, significantly older than I and were very accomplished, in their own right. As I listened to this man berate my colleagues, I was astounded that no one said a word in their own defense. I felt terrible for them. This man was turning accomplished people into impotent victims of verbal and psychological abuse. At the end of his diatribe, this individual asked if anyone had any comments. No one moved. I decided something had to be done, so I raised my hand. I said, "Perhaps if the presenter was less condescending and more respectful of the class, then the people here would be more receptive to his message." Stunned silence. Who was this young little whippersnapper to challenge an authority figure?

During the break, one by one, people came over to thank me for stating what they were thinking. I felt proud of myself for standing up to authority, but sad for my colleagues. Why did they not insist on being treated with dignity and respect? I thought about this for the next couple of weeks and remembered a concept I had been teaching in a course on social psychology called the "diffusion of responsibility." This theory basically states that people's inaction is based on their assumption that someone else will take care of the situation. When nothing happens, they justify that it was not their responsibility in the first place, so there is no guilt.

There are times when I bump into a former client and ask how things are going. On one such occasion, the client told me that her son, who had also been a client, was doing okay, but not great, and that her marriage and family problems had escalated. As I ended the conversation and headed to my car,

I was struck once again with guilt. Had I done enough for this client and her family? Should I have done something differently? I dwelled on it the entire ride home. I allowed myself to perseverate, but I gave myself a time limit. I could obsess about it until I got home, at which point I would stay in my car and listen to a cheerful song. Then, I would be able to go inside my home and become a functional—and guilt-free—husband to my wife and father to my children.

A note to readers struggling with unresolved guilt . . .

After conducting research on the topic of guilt, I discovered ideas as to how people can deal with guilt. The first realization came after receiving submissions of items for my survey from students, colleagues, and close friends. Writing down everything that can possibly cause guilt is so overwhelming that it becomes therapeutic. This may sound strange, but hear me out. When you see the enormity of the possible things to feel guilty about, you come to the realization that nobody would be able to survive if they shouldered all the burden of their guilt. You learn to accept that there are things in the past that cannot be changed. There are other things that we can become more conscious of and better ourselves through this newfound awareness, and we can make our relationships more meaningful.

Learning about prosocial behaviors through the many valuable experiments found in the discipline of social psychology has certainly brought this self-awareness to a whole new level. I have been teaching social psychology for about eight years now, and probably I am assumed to be extremely self-aware as a result, but we all slip up at times.

To help people overcome guilt feelings, I would like to offer a few practical tools to deal with something I call a constant: guilt. It is always there. Sometimes it is more conscious and sometimes less so. But it is there. Circumstances, life events, and relationships may bring up unresolved guilt.

Prepare yourself

With the knowledge that guilt is a constant, we are better prepared to deal with it when it tries to run us down, just like a fast-moving vehicle. If we're on the highway and a car is coming at us very fast, we can anticipate the potential danger and perhaps move over to another lane or slow down. When we can anticipate situations that trigger guilt, we can employ a similar defense. Pull over and make it conscious.

For example, my friend Linda knows that whenever she spends the holidays with her family, her mother will make some sort of comment about going back to college. This is a trigger point for Linda who dropped out of college in order to pursue another interest that never quite came to fruition. Linda knows that her mother will say something, so she can prepare her defense. Just like anticipating that fast-moving car, Linda can anticipate this huge oversized truckload of guilt barreling toward her. She can sidestep this guilt truck by either reducing the amount of time spent with her parents, going to therapy with her parents, or accepting the fact that they will probably not change much.

Laugh about it

Another way that we can deal with our guilt feelings is through humor. When we take ourselves lightly, the burden of guilt shifts to another remote part of the brain. If Linda were to develop a light-hearted response when her mother makes a "going back to college" reference, she could say "College is overrated. The degree is just an IOU for a lifetime of student loans!"

In other words, if we don't let ourselves take things too seriously, don't immediately condemn ourselves for being less than perfect, we have a chance at a better, more-informed view. Guilt thrives in black and white/right and wrong perspectives. Don't buy in to the temptation of guilt. Give yourself some leeway, brush yourself off, and move on.

Take responsibility

Taking responsibility means owning up to specific wrongdoings. Writing a handwritten apology about a specific wrongdoing can be powerful. Many clients have shared with me that they were able to move on more quickly after writing an apology.

I also emphasize to clients the importance of being genuine. I typically role-play with clients to practice how to take responsibility in a meaningful way. I help them construct a genuine forgiveness letter. We might even role-play a face-to-face conversation. Our nonverbal messages are sometimes more powerful than our verbal apologies.

If you own guilt, you need to get rid of it. If you have wronged someone in the past, you must make amends to whatever degree you can. For example, a previous client, Jim, was in a relationship that lasted several months. Jim had a quick temper and said some things to his partner, Carol, that were particularly hurtful. After Carol broke down, they broke up. Jim immediately felt very bad about the things he'd said and wanted to put the guilt away by apologizing to her. However, Carol did not accept it. Jim could not understand. Here he was, acknowledging his wrongdoing, yet he could not get

Carol to forgive him. During our sessions, I helped Jim realize that Carol was simply not ready for his apologies—it was too soon.

Forgiveness is a process that takes time. Sometimes people will never forgive you for the things that you did to wrong them. That's okay. It may cause you to feel guilty, but as long as you atone for your behavior at the appropriate time and with the appropriate intentions, you will eventually come to "disown" that guilt.

Obviously, we are discussing guilt as it pertains to minor misdeeds. The guilt of a rapist or murderer, on the other hand, should probably plague the perpetrator for many years. There are many cases of rape where the rapist attempts to make amends with his victims, and it causes more damage than good. A criminal should apologize to the victims but should never expect their apology will be accepted. They will have to own their guilt.

Help others

Too often, people rationalize their misdeeds, figuring their behavior is no different than the next guy's. This rationalization can lead us to falsely attribute the wrongdoing to something beyond the power of humankind. We can rise above the "I'm only human" excuse.

Take Randy, for example. He was backing out of a parking spot and accidentally scratched the car next to his. He thought for just a second that perhaps he should leave a note for the car owner, assuming responsibility for the repair. However, he quickly removed that thought and replaced it with another.

"This probably happens to everyone," he rationalized. "Why should I be the one who pays for the damage?" Taking ownership of your actions from the start makes it easier to follow the high road next time. It might even encourage others to do the same if they are in a similar predicament.

When teaching my social psychology class, I usually present these moral dilemmas to my students in an effort not only to make them aware of basic social psychology concepts but to make them better humans. We discuss the Bystander Effect, made popular by the infamous Kitty Genovese incident where 38 witnesses stood by and watched Kitty's murder, waiting for someone else to take action.

One of my students mentioned how when she was driving home after class she saw a man slumped over a bench by a bus stop. She pulled over, ascertained he was drunk, and then called a local organization for the homeless. Taking the action, she said, made her feel less guilty.

A note to clinicians dealing with unresolved "therapist guilt" . . .

Therapists suffer from guilt just as much as the next person, maybe even more so. After all, we listen to people's guilt for a living and triggers of our own shortcomings are all over the place. When we hear our clients' stories there is an unavoidable counter-transference that occurs.

Whether it is a client feeling that they made a poor choice in a relationship, a college pursuit, career, or whatever, guilt abounds.

Therapists will probably always debate how to deal with their guilt. There is no single right answer; however, dealing with our own guilt is essential. We must strive to process our experience in order to be of most value to clients who turn to us for support. Below I share with you a few techniques I've learned to be useful in accepting and transforming feelings of guilt.

Practice mindfulness
Mindfulness, the new wave for therapists, allows therapists to be situated in the present, calmly acknowledging thoughts, feelings, and bodily sensations. This approach can be very useful when therapists are dealing with their own personal guilt. Being aware in the moment helps us recognize our emotions, enabling us to move through our feelings, including guilt. I have begun to practice mindfulness techniques on a more frequent basis and encourage other therapists to do the same. Our lives are very fast-paced, and mindfulness helps us slow down and perceive things in a healthier way.

Keep a journal

Therapists sometimes find it helpful to keep a private journal where they record thoughts and feelings that pertain to their work with clients. The simple act of writing can be cathartic. But equally therapeutic is reading over your journals. We can learn from past mistakes as well as remind ourselves of techniques that worked well, and ones that weren't so successful. Writing helps take your feelings of guilt outside of your head, letting you learn from your hits and misses.

Take a break

There is no rule that states that therapists cannot cancel appointments. In fact, if you feel that you are unable to be "present" for your clients during therapy, it would be quite unethical to go about your normal schedule when you are dealing with feelings of unresolved guilt. As long as you don't make it a regular habit, cancelling appointments is sometimes necessary. Many therapists work late hours and weekends. We need to recharge in order to be of most value to others.

Get peer support and supervision

Everyone needs support. Social psychologists often talk about the need to belong. Whether you belong to a church group, a bowling group, or some other social group, we need to connect with others in meaningful ways.

Therapists especially need that support, because therapy can be a lonely profession. We are with people all day long, listening to their problems and being there for them. But we rarely have the opportunity to talk about our reactions, emotions, or concerns that accumulate over the course of a workday.

It does not matter how seasoned a therapist you are. Even if you have been practicing for thirty years, you can't—and shouldn't—go it alone. We need the support of our supervisors and colleagues to help keep our perspective and stay in tune with our own personal development.

Sometimes therapists are afraid of their supervisor's reaction, so they hold back sharing very personal feelings that are guilt-related. By not sharing your feelings, you are doing a disservice to your clients and to yourself. If you feel uncomfortable being fully upfront with a particular supervisor, it might be time to find a new one!

There are specific situations in which therapists can become paralyzed by feelings of guilt to the point that it impacts their ability to practice. Saying the wrong thing to a couple, making a recommendation impulsively, having a reaction to something you are personally struggling with, or dealing with the aftermath of a suicide can be paralyzing.

Recently, I have become more aware of the ramifications of suicide and the guilt that families face, along with the therapist. This could possibly be the ultimate manifestation of therapist guilt.

Many of my colleagues consider me an expert in suicide risk assessment, but it is not a title I enjoy. Over my career I've had to call parents of children as young as seven to alert them to their child's suicidal plans. I've had to file emergency petitions to have children admitted into the ER for a psychiatric evaluation. The reality is that people are suffering terribly.

Having counseled more than my fair share of suicidal people and seeing the unfortunate aftermath of a completed suicide has been devastating, to say the least. I have been at a loss for words, but the truth is there is not much that you can say to a family member of someone who has just killed himself. Many therapists feel guilty that they do not have the right words to say to a family suffering from the aftermath of a suicide. Most are afraid even to make the call to offer condolences.

The reality is that both family members and mental health professionals have a healthier outcome when they discuss their feelings openly. Support groups are very helpful in getting people to see that they are not alone in their feelings. It's a way to learn coping strategies and relieve the isolating feelings of guilt.

In conclusion, I have shared with you tales of therapy with the hope that my readers will be more attuned to what happens in therapy from both the clients' and the therapists' perspectives.

Some clients get better as a result of our interventions. Others do not. Guilt is a natural byproduct for all of us, but we can consciously choose to let it go.

Danish philosopher Soren Kierkegaard wisely wrote, "Life can only be understood backwards, but it must be lived forwards." The human condition is complex. Therapists—and most people, for that matter—attempt to explain life from what they have experienced. We must just keep on going. We can pause and reflect, but we can never completely stop our quest for knowledge learned from our past experiences. The stories you have read represent my new understanding of the very complex species we refer to as humans.

213

ACKNOWLEDGMENTS

I would like to first express my sincere thanks to all the clients who have shared their personal stories with me. They have given me the ultimate gift. They have exposed their vulnerabilities, articulated thoughts that they may have never shared with anyone before, and, perhaps most importantly, bravely entrusted themselves to another human being who has his own set of flaws and vulnerabilities. My care for them has been genuine, and my respect goes beyond their mere words. It is a true appreciation of each person as whole, unique, and worthy individuals.

I would like to thank the following individuals who have taken time to read over some of the content of this book. Those individuals who provided me valuable feedback include (in no particular order) Gali Kramer, Ellie Kramer, Shua Frank, Adam Edelman, my Writing for Psychology Class at Stevenson University, and the amazing 2017 AP psychology class at Beth Tfiloh.

A special thanks goes to my editor, Victoria Lasin. Victoria has encouraged me throughout the entire process and provided invaluable feedback that has made this work such a pleasant experience for me and, hopefully, the reader.

Since 2013, Stevenson, where I have served as a professor of psychology, has been my home away from home. Dr. Jeff

Elliott, the department chair for psychology has been so warm and welcoming, as have been my colleagues at Stevenson. I also would like to thank the many students whom I have had the privilege to teach.

I have never thanked him personally, but there is one man who fascinated me and turned me on to the field of psychology. In 1992, I took my first psychology course at Miami Dade Community College with a professor named Raul de la Cruz. The course was called *The Individual in Transition.* It was one of the most exciting courses I have ever taken. I looked forward to each and every class. Professor de la Cruz, with his quick wit and wisdom, truly inspired me to want to teach, "de la Cruz" style.

My graduate training took place at Miami Institute of Psychology, Albizu University. The many professors who gave of their time and energy in guiding their students all deserve recognition. A special shout out goes to Dr. Carmen Roca, my first supervisor, of whom I have very fond memories and great respect.

Dr. Norman Goldwasser deserves much credit. He has reminded me, on more than one occasion, of how my father influenced his decision to enter the field of psychology, and he in turn ended up supervising me while I was at school in Miami—the great circle of life. I thank him for his support.

In 1999, I began an internship in South Florida. The internship director was Dr. Arlene Huysman, of blessed memory, who always had an inspirational word to say whenever she would see me in the halls. Dr. Felicia Tralongo was an excellent supervisor who helped me out with some very challenging clients. I thank you both.

Clinical supervisors over time have provided me with different perspectives, as well as some rather challenging clients, and I would like to acknowledge Dr. Patti Friedman, Dr. Gabriel Newman, and Dr. David Michelson for all of their encouragement and wisdom.

My experiences in the city schools have influenced and framed a fresh perspective on how to deal with the child and adolescent population. For close to fourteen years I had the privilege of serving these students whose stories inspired a good deal of this book. I would like to thank Dr. Michael Oidick and Beckie Milburn for their supervision and encouragement.

My father is a true inspiration to me. An accomplished psychologist in his own right, he has been a constant source of knowledge. I wish him many more years of health and happiness from his children, grandchildren, and great-grandchildren. My mother has always provided the much-needed emotional support to help get me through difficult times. Although she has no official degree in psychology, her patience and ability to listen make her deserving of an honorary doctorate in psychology, which I proudly bestow on her.

My in-laws have always stood behind me and have defied the age-old negative stereotypes about in-laws. Thank you for your support as well.

My siblings, family members, and friends comprise too long a list to name individually. Consider yourselves thanked. To the many teachers, professors, and rabbis whom I had the privilege of learning from, I thank you as well.

My children have always consulted me with their literary questions. They also serve as a constant reminder to me that family comes first. This is why I did most of my writing in the summer while they were away, so I could be available during the year to attend their plays, parties, sports games, and, yes, help them with their essays. Thank you Tehilla, Dovid, Meir, Akiva, Tamar, and Shalva. I love you all!

My wife, Chaya, is the rock and glue of our family. Always remaining positive even during difficult times, you are a true inspiration to me and to everyone who is privileged to know you. I love you very much, and I thank you for your encouragement and support in this journey we call life.

I would like to especially thank Ruth Schwartz, also known as the Wonderlady and my book midwife, who worked her wonders and helped *birth* this book. From the beautiful cover design to the layout and the other details that go into publishing a work such as this, Ruth has been there for me. I am eternally grateful.

Lastly, I must give thanks to the one above. For without God's support and master plan, all of what I have accomplished would never be.

To the Reader,

It is my sincere hope that you gained something from reading *The Guilt Trap*. It has been a dream of mine to publish meaningful stories that almost everyone can relate to in some way.

As I mentioned in the Introduction to this book, I had an entirely different intention when I sat down on that very first day of writing. On my way to work that day, I brought a huge pile of surveys that I had received from my original research and creation of the guilt scale. My intention was to organize the data and plot it onto some fancy graph. As I read through some of the comments in the "optional feedback" section, I realized that the feedback seemed more valuable than the data. It was for this reason, I decided to write *The Guilt Trap and Other Tales of Psychotherapy*. I do not regret it and no—I do not have any **guilt** for letting those surveys lay dormant in a box. After all, it was a pilot study.

Since I value your feedback please take some time to share with me your thoughts about this book and if you are willing, tell me which story or stories spoke to you and why. You can write me at theguilttrap@gmail.com or visit me at doctor-jonny.com.

Once again, I thank you for reading my book. Whether you are a clinician, a clinician in training (CIT) or a fan of this genre, I hope you gained as much from reading this book as I did from writing this book.

With appreciation,
Dr. Jonathan M. Lasson

www.ingramcontent.com/pod-product-compliance
Lightning Source LLC
Chambersburg PA
CBHW070924030426
42336CB00014BA/2526